THE REALITIES OF AFFIRMATIVE ACTION IN EMPLOYMENT

Barbara F. Reskin

American Sociological Association
Washington, DC

Cite as:
Reskin, Barbara F. 1998. *The Realities of Affirmative Action in Employment*. Washington, DC: American Sociological Association.

For information:
American Sociological Association
1722 N Street NW
Washington, DC 20036-2981
(202) 833-3410
E-mail: publications@asanet.org
Website: www.asanet.org

Library of Congress Catalog Card Number: 98-073324

ISBN 0-912764-36-8

Cover design by Anna Rosich

ABOUT THE ASA

The American Sociological Association (ASA), founded in 1905, is a non-profit membership association dedicated to serving sociologists in their work, advancing sociology as a scientific discipline and profession, and promoting the contributions and use of sociology to society. As the national organization for over 13,000 sociologists, the American Sociological Association is well positioned to provide a unique set of benefits to its members and to promote the vitality, visibility, and diversity of the discipline. Working at the national and international levels, the Association aims to articulate policy and implement programs likely to have the broadest possible impact for sociology now and in the future.

THE SYDNEY S. SPIVACK PROGRAM IN APPLIED SOCIAL RESEARCH AND SOCIAL POLICY

The Sydney S. Spivack Program in Applied Social Research and Social Policy, one of ASA's core initiatives, is a multifaceted effort to advance the uses and contributions of sociology to social policy. Through policy briefings, special research workshops, community initiatives, and fellowship opportunities, the Program links sociological knowledge to social policy; promotes social policy based on sound sociology; and provides relevant social research on a timely basis.

To Herb Costner, Joan Huber, and Stan Lieberson in gratitude for their mentoring.

TABLE OF CONTENTS

PREFACE

A book that brings social science knowledge to bear on issues of affirmative action is long overdue. Just a cursory reading of any newspaper or listening to radio or television commentary makes clear that this is a public policy topic more frequently charged with "heat" than "light." *The Realities of Affirmative Action in Employment* seeks to diffuse the rhetoric by adding the perspective of systematic empirical study.

As the title implies, *The Realities of Affirmative Action in Employment* is a project grounded in what we know about affirmative action. As a matter of public policy, affirmative action in employment evolved over several decades to address discrimination and to prevent its occurrence. Anti-discrimination laws were themselves insufficient to deter discrimination; thus, affirmative steps were necessary to create a "level playing field" and a system of employment where merit in hiring, promotion, and pay could prevail.

This book is about affirmative action in employment, how it works, and what impact it has had on employees, employers, and the public. Early on in the book, we learn that affirmative action is formally mandated for only a small proportion of employers and firms. The book, however, goes beyond where affirmative action may be technically required and considers more generally the impact of affirmative action in setting norms and standards of practice throughout the workplace.

In keeping with the goals of this project, *The Realities of Affirmative Action in Employment* was produced with an assiduous dedication to empirical research. The project sought to take the commonplace assumptions of proponents and opponents of affirmative action and ferret out myth from reality based strictly on scientific data and research. Also, it is comprehensive in its scope: The book takes into consideration the experiences and perspectives of employees who are the targets of affirmative action, other employees, all employers, and the public. It also examines the costs and benefits to organizations and firms.

As the Introduction makes clear, the project began with a workshop on "Social Science Perspectives on Affirmative Action" planned and convened by the American Sociological Association on June 27-29, 1996. As one of the key initiatives in ASA's Spivack Program in Applied Social Research and Social Policy, the workshop was dedicated to examining social policy through the lens of social science in this arena. Over the course of three days, 16 social scientists identified significant pieces of research and scrutinized findings and their implications for understanding affirmative action. Through background memoranda and face-to-face exchange, workshop participants started the process of identifying what we know about affirmative action and its outcomes and where we still need more research. Their own professional understanding of different streams of research helped to shape the work of this project and the subsequent conclusions in the book.

It took a skillful leader and rigorous scientist to make the project blossom and come to fruition in a volume. For that, Barbara Reskin deserves special commendation and thanks. Her own professional accomplishments in the areas of work and occupations, and race and gender made her a natural team leader for the workshop and the subsequent report writing. Her strong commitments to communicating research to policymakers, to careful presentation of data, and to intellectual rigor showed throughout this project. She worked creatively and doggedly on multiple drafts, bringing fresh insights to diverse strands of work, following up on new research, and checking and rechecking findings. She also responded with openness to reviews from workshop participants, ASA staff, and the Spivack Advisory Committee as well as from anonymous peer reviewers.

The result is *The Realities of Affirmative Action in Employment*. As discussions and debate continue about how best to reap the benefits of a diverse workforce, it is worth reading and rereading.

Felice J. Levine
Executive Officer

x

ACKNOWLEDGMENTS

This volume is the brain child of Felice Levine, Executive Officer of the American Sociological Association, whose commitment to bringing policy-relevant sociological knowledge to the American public persuaded me to carve out time from my research to discover the realities of affirmative action. Over the 26 months it took to bring Felice's idea to fruition, she provided every kind of support, short of holding my impatient collaborators on other projects at bay. Throughout this project several other ASA staff people made vital contributions. Carla Howery helped to organize the workshop that marked the beginning of the project, and was invariably good humored and encouraging when I was ill tempered and discouraged. In addition to the useful comments on countless drafts by Felice and Carla, I am grateful for the reactions of the Advisory Committee for the Spivack Program in Applied Social Research and Social Policy when the manuscript was still in its infancy.

When I ran out of steam and time after the fourth draft, Roberta Spalter-Roth spelled me, dividing a long, dense manuscript into chapters, weeding out superfluous facts, and drafting chapter summaries. Although I went on to write two more drafts, Roberta's reconstruction was important in shaping the final version, and some of the few colorful expressions in an otherwise fairly dry tome are Roberta's. Katherine Rosich worked days, evenings, and weekends during the final phase before publication, reading and reacting to substantive content before the manuscript was set in stone, checking references and errant cites; and in general, trying to make an honest woman out of me. Bringing design talent to the project, Karen Gray Edwards set and reset type. Other ASA staff whom I cannot name but to whom I am grateful helped to make this book a reality.

I am pleased to acknowledge the generosity of Faye Crosby for help at the outset of the project, especially for sharing a then-unpublished copy of her coauthored book on affirmative action. Helen Norton of the

National Partnership for Women & Families gave me important comments on the manuscript and then quick replies to repeated appeals for legal information. (Helen is now at the Civil Rights Division, Department of Justice.) I am grateful to Wayne Santoro for sharing his considerable expertise on affirmative action while acting as my research assistant on this project. I thank Naomi Cassirer, Amy Hasenkamp, Julie Kmec, and Debra McBrier for research assistance; Dolores J. McGee for editorial assistance; and Deborah J. Merritt and Lowell L. Hargens for enduring countless discussions of affirmative action.

I am indebted to William Bielby, Paul Burstein, Joan Huber, Marylee Taylor, and three anonymous reviewers for their close reading of and helpful comments on earlier versions of this book. I owe particular thanks to Thomas Pettigrew, Stephen Steinberg, and one anonymous reviewer for taking issue with much in the penultimate version. Although I doubt that any will be satisfied with my revision, the intelligent and impassioned criticisms from both sides of the fence pushed me to rethink the issues and to re-examine the evidence in order to justify what some viewed as an overly nonpartisan and others as an overly partisan account.

Just as the public holds varied views on affirmative action, so too do the colleagues I thank in the above paragraphs. An acknowledgment, therefore, does not signify agreement with any—and certainly not all—of my conclusions. Nor are those I thank responsible for any errors in this volume; any errors are solely my own.

Barbara F. Reskin

INTRODUCTION

Affirmative action in employment is among the most politicized social reforms of the second half of the twentieth century. The very term conjures up contradictory images: equal opportunity, reverse discrimination; unfair competition, a level playing field; diversity, quotas. While public policies of any scope and significance have avid supporters and opponents, affirmative action appears to have been beset by more than its fair share of controversy.

One reason for the controversy is that there is little attention to the reasons why affirmative action exists. Affirmative action came into being because sex and race discrimination are everyday occurrences in America's places of work. Regardless of whether discrimination results from employers' and managers' stereotypes and biases or from their doing business as usual, it exacts a high price on minorities, women, the employers who practice it, and American society. It is this everyday discrimination that affirmative action policies and practices are designed to prevent.

Another reason for this controversy is that few Americans understand what affirmative action in employment actually entails, which employers are obligated to practice it, and what its effects have been. One-third of the white respondents to a recent *New York Times*/CBS poll admitted that they were not sure what affirmative action meant (Steeh and Krysan 1996, p. 129). It is likely that many of the other two-thirds who thought they knew have it wrong.

Part of the confusion over the realities of affirmative action stems from the fact that its particulars depend on the context. What is true about formally mandated affirmative action in education or in government procurement programs often does not apply to affirmative action in employment, the focus of this volume. Even with respect to employment, the specifics entailed in mandatory affirmative action depend on the source of the mandate. A series of presidential orders requires some forms of affirmative action by Federal contractors and Federal agencies. Federal law authorizes courts to order certain types of affirmative actions for employers who have been found guilty of employment discrimination. In addition, the Supreme Court permits employers to pursue certain voluntary affirmative action efforts. Thus, affirmative action is not a single policy but a set of processes and practices that have evolved over three decades and share the goal of actively preventing discrimination.

Exacerbating the confusion is the fact that affirmative action has become a political football. People whose primary objective is to use affirmative action as a rallying cry—to arouse indignation, get voters to the polls, or sell books—have no incentive to accurately describe this complex beast. The politicization, misconstruction, and sheer complexities of affirmative action breed confusion and— since what is at stake are jobs, promotions, and earnings—resentment.

Misunderstanding and resentment make for interesting politics, but they do not foster rational public discourse. The object of examining the realities of affirmative action is to provide a foundation for informed public discussion and decisionmaking. This volume has drawn on a large number of scholarly studies to synthesize what social science has learned about affirmative action in the employment context and the implications of this knowledge for sound social policy.

This book began with a working group of social scientists convened by the American Sociological Association in June 1996. Group members brought expertise in organizations' behavior; the workings of labor markets; human resource and employment policies; race, gender, and ethnic inequality; employment discrimination; politics; social policy; and public opinion. Although working group members approached affirmative action quite differently in their own scholarship, the research record convinced workshop participants on the following points: First, on-going employment discrimination against minorities and women necessitates concerted efforts to check discrimination. Second, affirmative action is effective in reducing discrimination against historically excluded groups. Third, by encouraging the formalization of personnel practices, affirmative action has helped replace cronyism with more objective procedures and policies that benefit most workers. Fourth, affirmative action as practiced in the United States today is much closer to Americans' values than the rhetoric would have us believe.

Based on a review of social science evidence, working group members noted both the specific and generalized impact of affirmative action in reducing employment discrimination. Its symbolic effects on the workplace cannot be minimized. Nevertheless, participants also concluded that for affirmative action to realize its potential to eliminate discriminatory barriers, it must be mandated for a wider range of employers, and more resources must be devoted to its implementation. The alternative—weakening affirmative action—would be a costly and dangerous experiment that the United States cannot afford. Of course, affirmative action is not a silver bullet that can end employment discrimination. It must be combined with other policies and programs such as increased educational opportunity and economic development.

This report draws on the expertise of working group members and on the breadth of social science literature on discrimination and affirmative action. The first chapter of this report defines affirmative action as actions, policies, and procedures designed to combat discrimination in the workplace and hence to equalize employment opportunity. The details of these actions, policies, and procedures depend partly on whether affirmative action is officially mandated by the federal government's contract-compliance program or a court decree, or whether it is a voluntary program. Chapter 2 describes the discriminatory practices that affirmative action was designed to overcome and the consequences of these practices. Chapter 3 presents research on the effects of affirmative action policies on minorities' and women's job opportunities. It shows that, when employers act in good faith, affirmative action has reduced discriminatory barriers to jobs. Chapter 4 examines what affirmative action practices are most effective. These include firm leadership; goals, timetables, and monitoring; and formalized personnel practices. Chapter 5 addresses the impact of affirmative action on members of groups not targeted for protection and on American commerce, and it summarizes public reactions to affirmative action. Chapter 6 brings the findings together and discusses their implications for U.S. equal employment policy.

Chapter 1

THE DEVELOPMENT OF AFFIRMATIVE ACTION IN EMPLOYMENT

WHAT IS AFFIRMATIVE ACTION IN EMPLOYMENT?

Affirmative action refers to policies and procedures designed to combat on-going job discrimination in the workplace. Like anti-discrimination laws, the goal of affirmative action is to make equal opportunity a reality for members of groups that have commonly been the object of discrimination. Unlike anti-discrimination laws, which provide remedies to which workers can appeal after they have suffered discrimination, affirmative action policies aim to keep discrimination from occurring. Affirmative action can prevent discrimination by replacing employment practices that are discriminatory—either by intent or default—with employment practices that safeguard against discrimination.

As it exists today, affirmative action grew out of civil rights laws, presidential executive orders, court cases, Federal implementation efforts, and human resource practices voluntarily implemented by employers. Since the practice as well as the meaning of affirmative action has evolved over time (Gamson and Modigliani 1987; Skrentny 1996), affirmative action is an often perplexing set of policies and practices rather than a single, synchronous policy that involves the same procedures for all employers.

5

Although affirmative action shares with anti-discrimination laws the goal of eliminating discrimination, it represents a break with the strategy of ending discrimination by outlawing it. Because affirmative action was spawned by the recognition that much discrimination results from employers doing business as usual, it requires employers to do more than refrain from actively discriminating—it entails proactive efforts to promote equal employment opportunities for groups traditionally subject to employment discrimination (Graham 1990, p. 42; Steinberg 1995). In departing from the strategy of outlawing discrimination, it shifts the responsibility for monitoring from victims of discrimination to employers who are in a position to eliminate discrimination.

As Chapter 2 shows, until the mid-1960s, job discrimination against women and men of color and white women was a matter of course. Sometimes race or sex discrimination involved intentional acts by employers, such as discarding applications from members of the "wrong" group or telling an employment agency to send only white men. But discrimination is also built into the way that firms recruit and promote workers. As we indicate below, employers' most common recruitment method was and still is to ask employees for suggestions. This practice tends to produce applicants of the same race, sex, and ethnicity as the existing workforce. It results predictably in the assignment of workers to jobs based on their sex and race. This job segregation, in turn, excludes people of color and white women from jobs with promotion ladders, which—along with subjective promotion practices—means that few have had the opportunity to advance.

The passage in 1964 of a Federal law banning discrimination in employment curtailed the most blatant forms of discrimination, but had little effect on the discrimination that stemmed from the ways that organizations went about recruiting, screening, and evaluating workers. Custom, habit, self-interest, and people's aversion to the risks that change entails all favor the status quo. In pursuing ostensibly neutral recruitment, hiring, and promotion procedures that were customary before the passage of anti-discrimination regulations, establishments continued to exclude groups of workers from many lines of work. Eliminating such forms of habitual discrimination requires employers to actively modify their personnel practices. These modifications, designed to ensure race- and gender-neutral employment practices, are a fundamental part of affirmative action.

WHAT ARE THE TYPES OF AFFIRMATIVE ACTION?

The history of affirmative action reveals a different impetus for each of the four major types: (1) presidential and gubernatorial executive orders requiring action by government contractors and subcontractors, (2) regulations requiring affirmative action by public employers, (3) court orders based on anti-discrimination law, and (4) employers' voluntary human resources policies. Although the four share an emphasis on procedures and practices that ensure fairness, their origins and legal status vary. The first of these—affirmative action required of government contractors—introduced the idea of affirmative action to the business community. As we shall see in the next section, however, this type of affirmative action applies to a very small segment of American business.

Affirmative Action Required of Federal Contractors

The requirement that Federal contractors take affirmative action has its precedent in a 1941 executive order barring race discrimination in the Federal government and war industries issued by President Franklin Roosevelt in response to blatant and ubiquitous race discrimination. However, the agency charged with enforcing the executive order, the Fair Employment Practices Committee (FEPC), was understaffed,

7

underbudgeted, and, most important, lacked the mandate to sanction violators. As a result, race discrimination remained entrenched in employment practices, including those of defense contractors (Stephanopoulos and Edley 1995).

In the late 1950s, President Dwight Eisenhower responded to widespread race discrimination by defense contractors by asking Vice President Richard Nixon to study its causes. In his report to Eisenhower, Nixon concluded that discrimination stemmed not from employers' desire to harm African Americans, but from their continuing use of the discriminatory employment practices that were customary during the country's era of legal race discrimination. In response to Federal contractors' disregard for anti-discrimination executive orders, Nixon recommended requiring contractors to engage in what he called "remedial" actions, and what we now know as affirmative action. Although Eisenhower did not act on Nixon's recommendation, the Vice President's realization that discrimination stemmed from firms doing business as usual survives in the logic of affirmative action.

In 1961, President John F. Kennedy took the first steps toward implementing affirmative action for Federal contractors. His Executive Order 10925 created a Committee on Equal Employment Opportunity and required Federal contractors to take affirmative steps—which he termed *affirmative action*—to ensure that they treated prospective and existing workers equally, regardless of race, color, or national origin (Graham 1992, p. 53). Three years later, under pressure from the burgeoning Civil Rights movement, Congress enacted the 1964 Civil Rights Act. Title VII made it unlawful for employers to fail to hire, discharge, or otherwise discriminate against any person in the terms, conditions, or privileges of employment because of their race, color, religion, sex, or national origin.

In 1965, President Lyndon Johnson's Executive Order 11246 mandated affirmative action by firms with large Federal contracts. To be eligible for a Federal contract, firms had to agree "not to discriminate against any employee or applicant for employment because of race, color, religion, or national origin, and to take affirmative action to ensure that applicants are employed and employees are treated during their employment without regard to race, color, or national origin" [(3 C.F.R. 169 202(1) (1974)]. President Johnson added sex to the list in 1967. Thus, to be awarded a Federal contract, employers had to agree both not to discriminate and to take affirmative action to ensure that they did not discriminate.

Executive Order 11246 established the Office for Federal Contract Compliance (later reorganized as the Office for Federal Contract Compliance Programs or OFCCP) within the U.S. Department of Labor. The OFCCP is charged with monitoring Federal contractors' compliance with the executive order. The affirmative action programs that the OFCCP oversees have been dubbed "contract compliance programs."

As President, Nixon issued an executive order that required firms with at least $50,000 in federal contracts and at least 50 employees to produce written affirmative action plans that included goals and timetables. Although requiring plans with goals and timetables was controversial, contractors had the discretion to set their own goals based on their analysis of the available labor force. The OFCCP leaves the specifics of contractors' affirmative action programs to them on the assumption that contractors are best able to design their own programs through trial and error.

In 1973, Congress passed the Vocational Rehabilitation Act which required government contractors to take affirmative action for qualified workers with disabilities. A year later, it passed the Vietnam Veterans' Readjustment Act which required contractors to take affirmative action in hiring and promoting Vietnam-era veterans. These programs have not drawn the political opposition that has plagued affirmative action based on race and, to a lesser degree, sex.

Under Executive Order 11246, Federal contractors and subcontractors must first conduct a self-analysis to determine the status of women and minorities in all parts of their organizations and discover the reasons for any substantial disparity between the representation of women and minorities in the labor pool of qualified workers and their employment.[1] Based on these self-analyses, contractors must eliminate any discriminatory policies or practices and take proactive measures such as recruitment, training, and outreach to ensure more equitable use of qualified minorities and women.

In addition, contractors must establish goals to increase the participation of qualified members of underrepresented groups and the time frame within which they expect to achieve their goals (Burstein 1995; Norton 1996, p. 41; Office of Federal Contract Compliance Program, hereafter cited as OFCCP 1998a). Contractors' goals must be based on the available pool of qualified individuals, and their timetables are to reflect the time frame within which they expect to achieve their goals (Norton 1996, p. 41). The rationale for requiring goals and timetables was part of President Nixon's original 1959 analysis: to encourage contractors to replace recruiting and hiring practices that had segregated women and non-white men to a few occupations with practices that created a level playing field for all prospective workers.

Although many commentators and members of the public equate goals with quotas, OFCCP regulations expressly forbid quotas or giving less qualified workers preference based on their sex or race (Stephanopoulos and Edley 1995, section 6.3). The regulations state: "In seeking to achieve its goals, a [contractor] is never required to (1) hire a person who does not have the qualifications needed to perform the job successfully; (2) hire an unqualified person in preference to another applicant who is qualified; or (3) hire a less qualified person in preference to a more qualified person" (OFCCP 1998a). Taking affirmative action means developing and executing "action-oriented programs designed to eliminate problems and . . . to attain established goals" (Title 41 C.F.R., chap. 60-2.13).

The OFCCP is charged with monitoring contractors' affirmative action efforts through compliance reviews. It does not penalize contractors who make genuine, but unsuccessful, efforts to reach their goals. Instead, it encourages them to try other strategies. Thus, the core of affirmative action for Federal contractors involves replacing discriminatory personnel practices with practices that are nondiscriminatory. Often this means formalizing previously informal personnel practices (Edelman 1992; Dobbin et al. 1993). Affirmative action required of Federal contractors by the executive order is generally regarded as a fairly weak program, because enforcement varies with the shifting political views of the executive branch of government and because sanctions have rarely been imposed (Fix and Struyk 1993, p. 179; Leonard 1994).

Presidential executive order 11246 and its amendments apply only to businesses that do a substantial amount of business with the federal government and, therefore, with the American people. In addition to insisting that such contractors provide equal employment opportunity, the executive orders require that they "take affirmative action to recruit, hire, and promote minorities and women" whenever those groups are underrepresented in the employer's workforce relative to the availability of qualified female and minority prospective workers in the labor pool (Burstein 1995). Estimates put the number of federal contractors and subcontractors required to practice affirmative action at about 3 percent of American firms in 1995 (Stephanopoulos and Edley 1995, section 6.2; U.S. Bureau of the Census 1995, table 858).[2] Importantly, however, the contractors tend to be large corporations that employ about one fifth of the nation's labor force (Stephanopoulos and Edley 1995).

11

In sum, executive orders by Presidents Johnson and Nixon make identifying and eliminating discriminatory employment practices conditions for winning lucrative Federal contracts. Contractors must design and pursue employment practices that ensure that the race, sex, national origin, and religion of qualified workers do not bar them from jobs.

Affirmative Action in Government Agencies

President Kennedy's 1961 Executive Order 10925 encouraged executive departments and government agencies to take "positive measures for the elimination of any discrimination . . . which now exists." President Johnson's 1965 Executive Order 11246 also prohibited Federal agencies from discriminating based on race, creed, color, or national origin and required them "to promote the full realization of equal opportunity through a positive continuing program in each executive department and branch."[3] The concept of "a positive, continuing program" was meant to encourage Federal agencies to engage in affirmative action to prevent discrimination. President Nixon's 1969 executive order held Federal agencies responsible for affirmative action by charging agency heads with establishing and maintaining "an affirmative program of equal employment opportunity." Initially the U.S. Civil Service Commission monitored agencies' compliance; since 1978, the EEOC has had that responsibility.

Reinforcing these executives' orders was the 1972 Equal Employment Opportunity Act, which reaffirmed nondiscrimination in Federal employment. While the 1972 law did not oblige Federal agencies to take affirmative action, it required them to take steps to encourage equal employment opportunity (DiPrete 1989, p. 199). These steps included elements that resemble those in successful affirmative action programs such as developing equal employment opportunity (EEO) goals and plans to achieve them; identifying underutilized talent; using recruitment

12

methods that reach the whole pool of job candidates; developing and fully utilizing employees' skills; cooperating with community groups, schools, and other employers to improve community conditions that affect employability; identifying target positions for which lower-level employees might be eligible; training lower-level employees to enhance their promotion opportunities; monitoring sex and race differences in time in grade; increasing the representation of women and minorities through recruitment at specific grade levels and in specific job ladders; and undertaking self-evaluation (Rosenbloom 1977, p. 81; DiPrete 1989, p. 200). Although the executive orders and the 1972 EEO Act did not use the term "affirmative action," they required the kinds of proactive efforts to prevent discrimination that are the essence of affirmative action. In the 1990s, approximately three million people worked in Federal agencies covered by these regulations.

In 1989, at least 35 states and the District of Columbia had executive orders or statutes requiring affirmative action in employment (Hill and Jones 1993). These regulations typically extend to all state agencies, including state universities and state contractors and subcontractors (Hall and Albrecht 1979, p. 28). A 1986 survey of cities and counties whose 1980 populations exceeded 100,000 indicated that more than four out of five required affirmative action in public employment (Nay and Jones 1989), and 60 percent of these included goals and timetables (Santoro 1995). Because the specifics of these state and local regulations and their enforcement vary greatly, it is not possible to estimate how many jobs they cover. However, in the mid-1990s, state and local governments employed approximately five million workers.

Court-Ordered Affirmative Action

A third type of affirmative action—that ordered by Federal courts—is based in Federal law. The 1972 Equal Employment Opportunity Act, an

13

amendment to Title VII of the 1964 Civil Rights Act, provides the statutory basis for court-ordered affirmative action. This amendment empowers Federal courts to include affirmative action among the kinds of relief they require of firms found guilty of discrimination [42 U.S.C. 2000e-5(g)(1)]. In other words, Federal courts can order employers whom they have found guilty of discrimination to adopt affirmative action.[4] Courts can also implement affirmative action as part of a negotiated settlement in a discrimination case through a consent decree (Rhode 1989, p. 184).

Court-ordered or court-approved affirmative action is an after-the-fact remedy for situations in which employers have discriminated. Because it is remedial rather than preventive, under restricted conditions court-ordered affirmative action may require employers to employ or promote (or unions to admit) set proportions or numbers of minorities or women. Essentially, to remedy proven discrimination courts may impose quotas.

Only under exceptional circumstances can courts impose quotas, however. In several decisions in the middle 1980s, the Supreme Court has permitted lower courts to order hiring and promotion goals for employers and unions proven guilty of having discriminated against minorities or women. In general, according to the High Court, Title VII of the 1964 Civil Rights Act outlaws quotas, except in cases of such egregious or persistent discrimination that no other remedy exists. Even in these cases, the Court has ruled that quotas must be temporary and "narrowly drawn" so that they do not constitute an absolute bar for employment or promotion among members of the majority group.[5] These stipulations are intended to ensure that court-ordered quotas impose the smallest possible burden on majority-group workers, while still ameliorating proven discrimination against the minority group. For example, the Supreme Court allowed a court to impose a quota for nonwhite membership in a sheet metal union that had repeatedly defied court

14

orders to stop discriminating against African Americans (*Local 28, Sheet Metal Workers v. EEOC,* 478 U.S. 421, 1986). The High Court's ruling has made quotas a rarity in affirmative action programs in employment.[6]

Voluntary Affirmative Action

A fourth type of affirmative action includes activities that employers voluntarily implement. Although the contents of employers' voluntary affirmative action programs depend on their particular circumstances, several practices are common to such programs (Vernon-Gerstenfeld and Burke 1985). This is because these practices are cost effective, pass muster by regulatory agencies, are perceived to reduce the likelihood of a discrimination suit, and have been widely accepted as good business practices (Martin 1991, p. 503; Dobbin et al. 1993). The typical components of voluntary affirmative action programs are race- and gender-neutral, while encouraging the race and sex integration of jobs, such as job advertisements that note that the company is an equal opportunity employer. Some programs train managers about the implications of affirmative action for their normal business practices; others reward managers for their affirmative action performance (Edelman 1992, p. 1546; Badgett and Hartmann 1995).

Although some employers voluntarily treat race or sex as "plus factors" in choosing among equally qualified candidates, employers' right to do so is restricted by EEOC guidelines and judicial rulings. Considering candidates' race or gender is permissible only as a temporary measure to address severe job segregation. In one of a few such cases, for example, the High Court permitted Santa Clara County's Department of Transportation to treat sex as a plus factor in selecting a female candidate for a job as dispatcher in view of the fact that all of the Department's 238 skilled blue-collar workers were male, and the County's plan called for placing women in three of 55 expected openings

15

over the coming year. The Court allowed the County's voluntary plan because it addressed an extreme situation without unduly or permanently harming the career prospects of male workers. However, Federal courts have invalidated race and sex preferences in voluntary plans that are not "narrowly tailored to remedy past discrimination" (e.g. *Quirin v. City of Pittsburgh* 1992; *Maryland Troopers Association v. Evans* 1993; *Black Fire Fighters Association of Dallas v. City of Dallas* 1995; *Koski v. Gainer* 1995).

There are no precise data on the prevalence of voluntary affirmative action in U.S. firms, but survey data suggest that some form of voluntary affirmative action is practiced by many more employers than the number who are required to take affirmative action by executive orders or the courts. Estimates of the prevalence of such efforts are mixed. Of 346 organizations in a 1989 national probability survey, 71 percent had affirmative action plans, almost one-fifth had an EEO or an affirmative action office, and most had created structures and rules that foster affirmative action or equal employment opportunity (Edelman 1992).[7] However, surveys conducted in the early 1990s of employers in Los Angeles, Atlanta, Boston, Detroit, and New York suggest that fewer than half of all American firms engage in affirmative action. Forty-five percent of the employers surveyed in the first four cities between 1992 and 1994 said they took into account either equal employment opportunity or affirmative action in hiring workers (Holzer and Neumark 1998), and 40 percent of 312 large firms in the New York-New Jersey-Connecticut metropolitan area that were surveyed in 1993 reportedly employed some form of affirmative action to recruit minorities, 28 percent did so to recruit women, 32 percent employed affirmative action in promoting minorities, and 24 percent did so for promoting women (Miller 1994, p. 12). Public and nonprofit organizations are more likely than for-profit firms to employ affirmative action procedures (Dobbin et al. 1993).

16

While precise information is not available on the proportion of employers who engage in affirmative action or on workers employed in such firms, fewer than half of workers believe their employer practices affirmative action. Forty-four percent of Americans workers were employed in firms that had an affirmative action program or made a special effort to hire minorities, according to a 1990 national survey of workers (Davis and Smith 1994).[8] Firms with contracts with the Federal government employ 22 percent of the civilian labor force (U.S. Department of Labor 1996, p. 1). Together these estimates imply that about one-fifth of employees work at companies that voluntarily engage in some form of affirmative action. There are no data on the proportion of voluntary plans that include race- or gender-conscious elements.

CONCLUSION

Affirmative action involves proactive employment practices whose object is to prevent discrimination. It encompasses presidential and gubernatorial executive orders, regulations affecting Federal and state agencies and contractors, court orders, and voluntary organizational policies. U.S. employers who are obliged to engage in affirmative action include state and Federal agencies, private employers holding large contracts with the U.S. government, and firms that have been ordered by courts to engage in affirmative action to remedy egregious violations of the law. In total, relatively few employers are required by the Federal government to practice affirmative action. Although many more do so voluntarily, more than half of American firms do not engage in affirmative action.

Private firms that do not hold large Federal contracts and have not been sued for violating Federal anti-discrimination laws have no obligation to practice affirmative action. Those that do so voluntarily are subject to Federal anti-discrimination laws that bar reverse discrimination; hence, they may not include quotas. They may treat sex or race as plus factors in choosing between qualified candidates only in order to redress substantial disparities in their workforces that result from past exclusionary practices, and only if they do not unduly burden members of majority groups. Since the proportion of employers who are required to do so is much smaller, the reach of mandated affirmative action is limited. In part, as a result, we will see in the next chapter that the conditions that necessitated affirmative action in the 1960s still exist in the 1990s.

Chapter 2

DISCRIMINATORY EMPLOYMENT PRACTICES AND JOB SEGREGATION: THE CHALLENGES OF AFFIRMATIVE ACTION

The goal of affirmative action is to end systematic employment discrimination against minorities and white women. Affirmative action addresses two forms of employment discrimination: job discrimination—the assignment of people to jobs based on their sex or race, which is also known as *job segregation*—and promotion discrimination. These types of discrimination exclude women of all races and minority men from the most rewarding jobs and concentrate them in jobs that others eschew. This chapter examines the extent to which workers are segregated into different and unequal jobs based on their race and sex. It then reviews research on the ways that discrimination gives rise to sex and race segregation. Finally, it shows how job segregation produces economic disparities between race and sex groups.

JOB SEGREGATION BY RACE AND SEX

The racial and sex segregation of jobs is so pervasive that it is likely to be invisible to many Americans. Most jobs in the United States have been racially and sexually segregated since their inception. People of

19

color have been relegated to society's worst jobs throughout our nation's history, and most employed white women have been segregated into low-paying, dead-end jobs. African-American men, for example, were excluded from most jobs as the United States industrialized. In fact, until World War II, firms and unions conspired to reserve almost all industrial jobs for white men (Steinberg 1995). State laws, custom, and employers barred women from many jobs, and until World War II, many employers required that women quit when they married (Kessler-Harris 1982). The legacy of these practices is a system of sex- and race-based segregation in the nation's workplaces that has survived for decades after Title VII of the 1964 Civil Rights Act made job segregation and employment discrimination illegal (Bielby and Baron 1984; Reskin 1993; Butler 1996).

Until Congress passed the 1964 Civil Rights Act, in much of the United States it was legal to use race or sex to assign workers to some jobs and exclude them from others.[9] Even where it was illegal, it was common practice. State and municipal laws against employment discrimination that existed before 1964 were rarely enforced (Norgren and Hill 1964). For example, in response to more than 19,000 recorded complaints of employment discrimination by African Americans across 12 states, Fair Employment Practice Commissions issued just 26 cease-and-desist orders (Graham 1990, p. 131). Employers hired and promoted whomever they pleased on the basis of race, sex, and personal connections as well as qualifications.

In hiring and promoting decisions, employers routinely took workers' color and sex into account. As a result, white men held most of the country's most desirable jobs. In 1940, for example, white men were 62 percent of the labor force, but were 84 percent of managers and 92 percent of workers employed in the skilled trades. In contrast, white women, who made up 29 percent of the labor force, were 14 percent of managers and less than three percent of craft workers; non-white men, who were six percent of the labor force, were just 1.7 percent of managers and five percent of craft workers; and non-white women, who were four percent of the labor force, were 0.6 percent of managers and 0.2 percent of crafts workers (Treiman and Terrell 1975, table 7.3).

Despite the passage of the 1964 Civil Rights Act, by 1970 white men had increased their monopoly of the most desirable white-collar and blue-collar jobs compared to 1960 (U.S. Bureau of the Census 1963, table 25; 1972, table 2). The discriminatory behavior of thousands of large corporations; tens of thousands of small employers; and local, state, and Federal governments excluded women and minority men from managerial and skilled blue-collar jobs during this period.

Although both sex and race segregation have declined in the past quarter of a century, in the 1990s workers' sex and race still affect the jobs they hold, with white men still overrepresented in the best-paying jobs. In 1996, almost 30 percent of white workers held managerial or professional jobs, compared to about one in five African American workers, and fewer than one in seven Hispanic workers (U.S. Bureau of Labor Statistics 1997, table 10). Being African American also reduces men's access to sales and clerical jobs (Gill 1989, p. 620). More than one-quarter of white and African-American women worked in administrative-service occupations (mostly doing clerical work), compared to nine percent of African-American men and six percent of white men. Being female also continues to restrict women's access to the best paying blue-collar jobs: Only two to three percent of African-American and white women held precision-production and craft jobs in 1994. Both sex and race affect whether workers hold service jobs: Almost one-fourth of African-American women and one in seven African-American men and white women held service jobs in 1990, compared to six percent of white men.

21

Researchers summarize the degree to which workers are segregated by sex and race into different occupations with the index of segregation. This measure is the proportion of workers in a sex or race group who would have to change occupations in order for that group to be distributed across occupations in the same way as a comparison group. In 1990, 29 percent of African-American and Hispanic men would have had to relocate in other occupations to be distributed across occupations in the same manner as white men. Fifty-four percent of white women, 58 percent of Hispanic women, and 60 percent of African-American women would have had to have held different occupations to be distributed across occupations in the same way as white men. Although there is no reason to expect workers in a nondiscriminatory labor market to be perfectly integrated across occupations, these levels of sex and race segregation substantially exceed what one would expect if employers assigned jobs without regard to workers' sex or race. These segregation indices are consistent with the conclusion that discrimination in job assignment and promotion—whether the result of intentional acts or customary business practices—is still common.[10]

According to recent research, female and male workers also tend to be segregated into different firms. For example, in the early 1980s, about two-thirds of men or women employed in banks with fewer than 100 employees would have to go to work in a different bank for the sexes to be integrated across all banks. About half of the female or male employees of food stores or real estate agencies would have to switch firms for the sexes to be integrated (Carrington and Troske 1994). Statistics for the 1990s show continued sex segregation across firms, even for workers who perform the same occupation. Sixty-four percent of male or female textile, apparel, and finishing machine operators would have to be employed at a different firm for women and men in this line of work to be integrated (Carrington and Troske 1998a, p. 453). Importantly, the

22

firms that employ men pay more than those that employ women (Carrington and Troske 1994; 1998a, p. 460).

Although the Federal government has traditionally offered minorities and white women wider employment opportunities than the private sector, in the middle 1990s female and minority workers remained underrepresented among professionals and overrepresented in clerical jobs and other lower-level positions (Stephanopoulos and Edley 1995). In state and local government, women are underrepresented in skilled blue-collar, protective-service, and administrative jobs; Hispanics and African Americans are underrepresented in administrative and professional jobs; and African Americans are also underrepresented in technical jobs (U.S. Bureau of the Census 1998).[11] Partly as a result of job segregation, women employed in state and local government average 81 percent of men's median salaries, African Americans earn 85 percent as much as non-Hispanic whites, and Hispanics earn 91 percent as much (U.S. Bureau of the Census 1998).

EMPLOYMENT DISCRIMINATION

Employment discrimination includes all work-related practices that treat people differently because of their sex, race, or national origin. It is a matter of deep public concern because it has led to the exclusion of entire groups from entire sectors of the work world. Like affirmative action, discrimination involves a variety of processes and practices. Prior to the passage of anti-discrimination laws, discrimination strongly curtailed the kinds of jobs that minorities and white women could hold. Entire industries and occupations were virtually off-limits to women of any race or ethnicity and to non-white men. People of color and white women were confined to a small number of occupations—occupations that tended to be low paying and dead-end.

23

In thousands of towns and cities, police departments and fire departments remained all white and male; women and minorities were forbidden to even apply. In grocery and department stores, clerks were white and janitors and elevator operators were black. Generations of African Americans swept the floors in factories while denied the opportunity to become higher paid operatives on the machines. In businesses such as the canning industry, Asian Americans were not only precluded from becoming managers, but were housed in physically segregated living quarters. Stereotypical assumptions that women would be only parttime or temporary workers resulted in their exclusion from a full range of job opportunities. Newspaper job listings were segregated by gender. Women also confronted other barriers to full inclusion: lower pay and fewer benefits than men, even when performing similar jobs; losing their jobs if they married or became pregnant; and sexual harassment on the job (Stephanopoulos and Edley 1995, section 2.1)

Although the anti-discrimination laws passed in the 1960s and 1970s have reduced job discrimination (Burstein 1985),[12] the evidence summarized below indicates that discrimination persists in America's workplaces. In part, this is because discrimination is not simply the result of deliberate attempts to discriminate. While some discrimination results from employers' active preference for one group over another, much of it stems from their other goals or from the tendency to continue to do things the same way as in the past. As Baron (1991, p. 115) observed, when founded, organizations adopt structures that "correspond to broader social understandings about how [they] ought to look and ought to be run." Thus, organizations established when race and sex segregation was legal and commonplace often continue to pursue practices that segregate

24

and discriminate, simply by doing business as usual.

Since employment discrimination is illegal, much of the evidence of its incidence is indirect. One type of evidence of different employment outcomes based on race and sex comes from discrimination complaints, discrimination litigation, "audit" studies, and statistical studies that show residual differences between group outcomes after the effects of other factors are taken into account. A second type of evidence is found in the reports made by employers to researchers about how race and sex affect their hiring practices. A third type is the prevalence of organizational practices that have discriminatory consequences.

DISPARATE TREATMENT AND DISPARATE OUTCOMES

A formal complaint of discrimination does not prove that an employer has discriminated. Nonetheless, the thousands of race and sex discrimination complaints filed each year with enforcement agencies, along with other evidence reviewed below, suggest considerable discrimination. Since 1965, women and minorities have filed nearly 1.5 million discrimination complaints (Blumrosen 1996, p. 4). In 1994, for example, state and local Fair Employment Practice Commissions received 64,423 complaints of employment discrimination, and the Equal Employment Opportunity Commission (EEOC) received more than 91,000 complaints, adding to its backlog of 73,000 cases (Leonard 1994, p. 24). Although we have no basis for determining how many of these complaints are valid instances of discrimination, the evidence presented in this chapter leaves no doubt that job discrimination is widespread.

Disparate outcomes that appear to stem from intentional discrimination have been uncovered by the Federal agencies charged with enforcing anti-discrimination laws. For example, in 1994 the OFCCP found that Provident Bancorp of Cincinnati had hired less qualified non-Hispanic whites in preference to African American, Hispanic, and Asian

25

applicants for jobs as tellers and general clerks (OFCCP 1998b). During an investigation of Smith & Wesson's Springfield, Massachusetts plant, the OFCCP discovered that Smith & Wesson had not hired a single one of the 1,600 women who had applied for production and craft jobs between 1985 and 1987 (U.S. Department of Labor, Employment Standards Administration, OFCCP 1995). Investigators found a similar pattern at Dart, Inc. Dart gave male applicants mechanical-aptitude tests for well-paying, semi-skilled jobs, while it gave female applicants manual-dexterity tests for low-paying, heavily female jobs. Between 1994 and 1995, GF Office Furniture turned down 336 qualified women for blue-collar entry-level jobs because of their sex (U.S. Department of Labor, Employment Standards Administration 1996).

The news media have given considerable attention to some of these charges. Racial barriers to promotion at Texaco drew enormous interest in 1996 when an executive released taped conversations in which senior executives spoke pejoratively of African Americans (who had sued for race discrimination) because it provided a rare glimpse into the white male inner circle. Insiders willing to admit to such blatant sex and race discrimination as that which occurred at Texaco are few and far between. But Texaco is hardly alone in its deliberate discrimination against people of color and white women. In 1996, a Federal jury found Circuit City guilty of systematically discriminating in promotions against African Americans employed at its corporate headquarters. Other corporations found guilty of race or sex discrimination in the 1990s include British Petroleum of the U.S., Burlington Industries, Canon Business Machines, Honeywell Corporation, Kimberley Clark, Lucky Stores, Marriott Hotels, Merrill-Lynch, and the Shoney's restaurant chain, to name a few (Duke 1993; White 1996).[13]

The results of a series of employment "audits" conducted in the early 1990s support the evidence from individual complaints and media

26

reports that employment discrimination is common. Employment audits compare the job-search outcomes of members of equally qualified pairs of applicants, only one of whom belongs to a minority group. The audits conducted between 1989 and 1992 indicate that employers who advertised jobs or recruited through employment agencies discriminated against minorities between one-fourth and one-fifth of the time.[14] These results underestimate the prevalence of discrimination because, as we will see below, discriminating employers often avoid recruiting methods that give minorities or white women the chance to apply. Thus, the audit studies address discrimination among employers whose recruitment methods are nominally open. The estimates of discrimination are based on more than 1,500 such audits—some of which paired African American and white testers, and some of which paired Anglo and Hispanic testers—that were conducted in Chicago, Denver, San Diego, and Washington, DC by the Urban Institute, the Fair Employment Council of Greater Washington, DC, and the University of Colorado (Cross et al. 1990; Turner, Fix and Struyk 1991; Fix and Struyk 1993; Kenney and Wissoker 1994).

The employment audits conducted in Washington, DC illustrate how discrimination can occur in each step of the hiring process. Of the pairs who applied for jobs advertised in *The Washington Post* and at employment agencies listed in *The Yellow Pages*, whites were slightly more likely than African Americans to obtain interviews, white interviewees were more than four times more likely than African-American interviewees to receive job offers, and the jobs offered to whites paid more than those offered to African Americans (Fair Employment Council 1992). In one case, the interviewer at a large Washington employment agency told an African-American female applicant that she would be called if a suitable vacancy opened. When her white audit partner applied to the same agency for similar employment, the agency coached

27

her on interviewing techniques and scheduled an interview at an upscale health and grooming firm; the firm offered her a job (Bendick 1992). The only audit study assessing sex bias found that when male and female applicants applied for jobs as waitpersons, high-price restaurants were substantially more likely to interview and to offer jobs to men, whereas low-priced restaurants, whose waiters earn significantly less, were more likely to interview and offer jobs to women (Neumark 1996).

EMPLOYERS' REPORTS OF EMPLOYMENT PRACTICES

Employers' reports about their own hiring practices attest to discrimination in America's workplaces. Private firms in Boston, Detroit, and Los Angeles studied between 1992 and 1994 hired more Asian and white applicants than African American and Latinos (Moss and Tilly 1996). Although these differences may partly reflect differences in qualifications, recent studies in several American cities have documented that employers' stereotypes about African Americans prompt them to discriminate against African American job applicants (Browne and Hewitt 1995; Bobo and Hutchings 1996; Bobo and Suh 1996; Kasinitz and Rosenberg 1996; Kennelly 1996; Wilson 1996, chap. 5; Moss and Tilly 1996). For example, an early 1990s study of the auto-parts supply industry in the Detroit metropolitan area revealed that temporary employment agencies help to keep firms segregated, sometimes at employers' requests. Agencies sent whites to firms in the suburbs and sent African Americans to African-American-owned firms or Detroit firms that employed many African Americans (Turner 1996, p. 36, note 18).

A survey of 185 Chicago employers conducted in 1988 and 1989 indicated that racial stereotypes routinely influence how employers fill entry-level jobs (Kirschenman and Neckerman 1991; Neckerman and Kirschenman 1991; Wilson 1996, chap. 5). More recent surveys in

Detroit and Los Angeles mirrored the Chicago results: 44 to 61 percent of employers viewed African-American men as lacking the motivation and the social skills that they felt their employees needed (Moss and Tilly 1996, p. 264). In explaining their discriminatory practices, some employers raised concerns about the reactions of customers or co-workers (Moss and Tilly 1996). For example, a Chicago employer of marketing representatives explained to a researcher who was studying hiring practices that "it makes [the job] more difficult when we put a African American in an all-white environment, and there's golf, and golf is generally a white bastion. We don't have a problem doing it, but I can't take an everyday African American and put him in" (Kirschenman 1996, p. 15).

Many Americans subscribe to unfavorable stereotypes of African Americans, Hispanics, and Asians, and of white women, although the content of race, ethnic, and sex stereotypes varies (Sniderman and Piazza 1993; Bobo 1997; Schuman et al. 1997; Sigelman and Tuch 1997). Whites tend to view African Americans as lazy, unintelligent, prone to violence, and insubordinate (Smith 1990; Bobo 1996; Wilson 1996, chap. 5). Latinos are stereotyped as unintelligent, prone to violence, and content to live on welfare, while Asians are stereotyped as hard to get along with (Ramirez 1988, p. 199; Smith 1990; Bobo et al. 1994, p. 117). Employers often cite racial stereotypes to justify their reluctance to hire minorities (Neckerman and Kirschenman 1991; Browne and Hewitt 1995; Bobo and Suh 1996; Kasinitz and Rosenberg 1996; Kennelly 1996). Race and sex stereotypes contribute to discrimination because employers make employment decisions as if their beliefs about groups apply to all members of the group (Bielby and Baron 1986). Consider the employers in a Brooklyn neighborhood who rejected African-American and Latino job applicants from the nearby housing projects. As one employer put it, "I don't discriminate . . . . But naturally you'd distrust somebody who

29

comes from a place like that" (Kasinitz and Rosenberg 1996, p. 191).

Sex stereotypes characterize women as uncommitted to their careers, emotional, mechanically incompetent, physically weak, and reticent (Williams and Best 1986; Fiske, Bersoff, Borgida, Deaux, and Heilman 1991; Heilman 1995). Although contemporary sex stereotypes may be less pejorative than race stereotypes, they nonetheless support women's exclusion from many occupations (Heilman 1995). Sex stereotypes that characterize women as uncommitted to their jobs, unable to make decisions, too emotional, and insufficiently aggressive have contributed to their underrepresentation in top management (U.S. Department of Labor, Office of Federal Contract Compliance Programs, Glass Ceiling Commission, hereafter cited as the Glass Ceiling Commission, 1995). In conjunction with the labeling of jobs as "men's work" or "women's work," sex stereotypes influence whether employers view female job candidates as qualified. This happens in blue-collar and managerial jobs customarily held by men. For example, when a utility company assigned women to customarily male power plant jobs during a 1983 strike, managers transferred them to food service and plant cleaning on the assumption that women lack the physical or mechanical skills to hold any other jobs (Reskin and Padavic 1988).

Whether or not a stereotype has any foundation in fact, its effect is to deny opportunities to members of negatively stereotyped groups by influencing the evaluations of job applicants and employees. Stereotypes lead to sex and race discrimination in hiring, promotions, and terminations by biasing employers' evaluations of job applicants and workers (Braddock and McPartland 1987; Pettigrew and Martin 1987). This evaluation bias occurs because employers' stereotypes or prejudices distort their assessments of workers or prospective workers. Stereotypes bias evaluations by ascribing to individuals undesirable characteristics, causing evaluators to disregard evidence that is inconsistent with their stereotypes, and lowering employers' expectations for members of negatively stereotyped groups (Nieva and Gutek 1981, pp. 69–81; Heilman 1984; Gerber 1989; Foschi, Lai, and Sigerson 1994). In lowering supervisors' expectations for minorities and women's performance, evaluation bias adversely affects performance through the loss of material and psychological support (Kanter 1977; Darley and Fazio 1980; Bell and Nkomo 1994, p. 24).

We see the effect of racial stereotypes when employers evaluate white workers more positively than equally qualified African-American workers (Kraiger and Ford 1985; Pulakos et al. 1989; Greenhaus, Parasuraman, and Wormley 1990, table 1). Evaluation bias against women is most likely in settings with few women, such as predominantly male nonmanagerial jobs (Sackett, DuBois, and Noe 1991, p. 266).

Discriminatory bias also occurs when employers hold minorities or women to different or higher standards than whites and men (Cox and Nkomo 1986; Holzer 1996). Recent surveys offer evidence that employers require different qualifications for women and men or for minorities and whites. For example, Chicago employers evaluating job applicants were more likely to judge women based on their personality and men on their education (Bills 1988, p. 84), and central-city firms that disproportionately hire African Americans are more likely than suburban firms to insist on specific credentials (Holzer 1996).

Although expressed stereotypes are at the heart of much of the discrimination that employers admit to, some emphasize a preference for a friend or crony (McGinley 1997). Since people's friends are likely to be of the same sex and race, the effect of cronyism is to disproportionately exclude women of all races and minority men. For example, an African American woman sued the Newport Naval Base for discrimination after two white men rewrote the job description to fit the qualifications of a "fishing buddy" (McGinley 1997).

31

DISCRIMINATORY PERSONNEL PRACTICES

Structural Discrimination

Much of the race and sex discrimination in America's workplaces is built into the ways that firms conduct business. This "structural discrimination" includes employment practices that are race- and gender-neutral on the surface, but whose effects are predictably discriminatory. We illustrate this with two common types of structural discrimination: employers' use of informal networks to recruit workers and requiring job credentials that are not necessary to a job.

The methods employers use to recruit workers often limit who learns about job openings and applies for jobs. The most common recruiting method—word-of-mouth recruiting—identifies job candidates through referrals by current employees (Marsden 1994; Miller and Rosenbaum 1997, p. 513). Word-of-mouth recruiting is popular because it is cheap: Current employees know what skills job candidates need, can vouch for candidates, and are more likely to help train workers they know.

However, word-of-mouth recruitment maintains the race, ethnic, and sex composition of a firm's workforce (Kasinitz and Rosenberg 1996, p. 188; Newman 996, p. 22; Reskin and McBrier 1998), largely because people's acquaintances tend to be of their same sex and race.[15] When employers fill jobs through informal networks, minorities and women do not learn about jobs for which they are qualified (Braddock and McPartland 1987), even when jobs are abundant and even in firms in their own neighborhoods (Kasintz and Rosenberg 1996, p. 189). For example, African Americans lost ground in the New York construction industry during periods of full employment because most contractors recruited through word-of-mouth (Waldinger and Bailey 1991). Like other discriminatory practices, word-of-mouth recruiting reduces the likelihood that employers will hire the most qualified candidates.

Recruiting workers through informal networks is less discriminatory the better integrated people of color and white women are across firms and throughout establishments' hierarchies.

Although posting jobs or advertising them in public media helps to reduce structural discrimination in employment, no more than 40 percent of job vacancies are formally advertised (Bendick and Egan 1988; Marsden 1994, p. 983); less skilled jobs for which members of disadvantaged groups often qualify are even less likely to be advertised (Braddock and McPartland 1987, p. 35).[16] However, advertising jobs circumvents the bias associated with the use of informal networks only if employers advertise in media that are visible to minority job seekers, and employers who advertise jobs often do so in newspapers that racial minorities are unlikely to see. According to Wilson (1996), among those Chicago employers who advertised job openings, two-thirds did so in neighborhood, ethnic, or suburban newspapers, papers African Americans rarely saw. Not surprisingly, employers who advertised in local newspapers were only half as likely to employ African Americans as those who advertised in metropolitan papers.

The ways that employers choose workers for particular jobs often open the door to discrimination. When employers lack accurate information about applicants, they are especially likely to base employment decisions on stereotypes, and yet employers tend to prefer their subjective impressions to objective indicators of future performance (Holzer 1996, pp. 83, 103; Miller and Rosenbaum 1997). For example, according to a 1994 survey of 3,347 private firms with at least 20 employees, employers attached the greatest importance to characteristics that are hardest to assess objectively such as applicants' attitudes, and the least importance to more objective measures such as years of schooling, tests administered during the interviews, and teachers' recommendations (Zemsky and Iannozzi 1995).

33

Evaluations are most subject to bias when the evaluation criteria are vague, ambiguous, or subjective (American Psychological Association 1987; Messick and Mackie 1989, pp. 49–50; Fiske and Taylor 1991), and in work settings in which majority-group members predominate (Kanter 1977; Sackett et al. 1991, p. 265). Although explicit criteria and objective measures of performance reduce the likelihood of evaluation bias and thus of employment discrimination (Ford, Kraiger, and Schectman 1986; Baron 1991, p. 124; Martocchio and Whitener 1992, p. 500),[17] subjective evaluation and vague criteria appear to be the norm. The impression a job candidate makes during the interview is of primary importance to many employers (Bills 1988; Zemsky and Iannozzi 1995; Miller and Rosenbaum 1997). Surveys of private firms in Los Angeles, Detroit, Chicago, and Boston in the late 1980s and early 1990s provide evidence of the exclusionary effect of subjective screening methods: When interviews were used as important screening devices, employment of African-American men was lower; when tests were used, African-American men's employment rates were higher (Moss and Tilly 1997; Neckerman and Kirschenman 1991).

Another form of structural discrimination can occur when employers require credentials that workers do not need to do the job. When required credentials are not necessary for job performance and requirements disproportionately exclude minorities or women, their effect is discriminatory. Yet employers often require skills or experience that workers do not need and that women or minorities are less likely than white men to have. An example is employers' insistence on unneeded educational credentials or job applicants' ability to lift heavy objects for jobs that rarely involve heavy lifting (Bielby and Baron 1986).

The Organization of Work

By designing jobs based on the assumption that one sex or the other will hold them, employers create structural barriers against women filling specific jobs—jobs that tend to pay better than customarily female jobs. For example, machinery and equipment used in customarily-male occupations are designed to accommodate men, often white men. Consequently, small women and some Asian men cannot operate them as safely or efficiently as averaged-sized white men. Some companies organize work such that workers rotate across different shifts—day, evening, and graveyard—thus excluding workers who must make regular childcare arrangements, who are usually female (Padavic 1991). These examples show that seemingly neutral aspects of work such as the structure of the equipment or the timing of shifts—because they assume that workers are male—tend to exclude women.

Structural Discrimination and Organizational Inertia

Structural discrimination persists because, once in place, discriminatory practices in bureaucratic organizations are hard to change. Organizational practices that were designed or evolved at a time when the labor force was mostly male and when African Americans, Hispanics, Asians, and Native Americans were confined to the worst jobs tend to persist in contemporary workplaces unless they are explicitly challenged.

Research on gender inequality in California state agencies shows the role of inertia in maintaining race and sex segregation. Younger state agencies which were established after public concern with workplace equity surfaced made greater progress in breaking down job segregation than did older agencies. The entrenched nature of discriminatory practices is illustrated by the fact that even organizations under court-ordered affirmative action that were supervised by court-ordered administrators have taken almost 20 years to achieve rather modest gains in minorities' and women's representation in jobs from which they had been excluded (Blumrosen 1996, pp. 10–19).

Organizations' resistance to change stems from an aversion to the risk associated with deviating from customary practices. As Barbara Bergmann (1996, p. 79) observed, when employers hire from groups that they already employ, they are on familiar terrain and hence confident in their decisions, whereas employers who have little experience with minority and women workers may feel unable to predict who is likely to be a good worker. Inertia in organizations' personnel practices is exacerbated by women's and minorities' absence from influential positions and by decisionmakers' lack of accountability for discriminatory outcomes. Given a tradition of discriminatory employment practices and no pressures to change, organizational inertia means that discrimination typically persists (Baron and Bielby 1985; Baron 1991, pp. 127, 134; Cohen, Broschak, and Haveman 1998, p. 39).[18]

In sum, some employers discriminate against workers based on stereotypes, prejudices, fears, or hostility toward members of a particular group. Sometimes employers make discriminatory decisions in anticipation of difficulties with prejudiced customers or employees. And often, discrimination is the inevitable result of employers' standard operating practices that disadvantage women and minorities. This last type of discrimination, termed "structural discrimination" by sociologists, includes practices that are ostensibly race- and gender-neutral but that have predictably discriminatory effects. The inertia typical of organizations preserves these practices, barring genuine pressures to change them.

Informal Workplace Practices

Discrimination also enters workplaces through informal practices. Even in organizations with formal policies against discrimination, informal practices can adversely affect minorities' and women's career opportunities. Foremost is minorities' and women's exclusion from informal networks or casual social relationships that are a primary source of help and through which valuable information is exchanged (Bell and Nkomo 1994). Exclusion from informal work groups can impair performance by censoring information that workers need in order to do their jobs, to acquire new skills, to learn about advancement opportunities, and to build trust with potential mentors (Pettigrew and Martin 1987; Bobo and Suh 1996, p. 36). Informal networks tend to be segregated by race and sex (Brass 1985; Ibarra 1992, 1993; Bell and Nkomo 1994, p. 40). One of the first African Americans in sales at Xerox recalled, for instance, that African-American salesmen's exclusion from informal networks meant that they did not have a chance to develop relationships with coworkers in which they could learn the organization's informal norms that mark one as an insider (Rand 1996, p. 70; see also Friedman and Deinard 1996).

Like informal networks, ties with mentors or sponsors also tend to be sex and race-segregated (Bell and Nkomo 1994, p. 30; McGuire 1998), and minority workers are less likely than white workers to have mentors (Cox and Nkomo 1991, table 2; but see Greenhaus et al. 1990, table 2). This means that minorities and women are disadvantaged at firms in which advancement depends on senior-level sponsorship. In describing work challenges they faced, female managers were more likely than their male counterparts to report that they lacked personal support (Ohlott, Ruderman, and McCauley 1994, table 3).

THE COSTS OF SEGREGATION AND DISCRIMINATION

The sex and race segregation of workers that results from employment discrimination comes at a high price. In concentrating women and minorities in occupations that pay less than their education, experience, and skills warrant, employment discrimination confines some Americans

37

to an economically marginal existence with little chance for escape (Erdreich, Slavet, and Amador 1996, pp. xii-xiii). Many factors contribute to sex and race differences in unemployment and underemployment, promotion rates, exclusion from top management, and earnings. Some particularly significant ones are differences in education, training, and experience as well as in geographic proximity to available jobs. But the evidence summarized in this chapter establishes that discrimination plays a consequential role.

By denying employment to some workers based on their race and sex and segregating others into jobs based on these characteristics, discrimination lowers the labor force participation and raises the unemployment rates of non-whites. It reduces the earnings of minorities and women, and disproportionately denies them the opportunity to acquire skills and to advance in their careers. In artificially restricting the productivity of millions of Americans, it accordingly depresses America's productivity.

UNEMPLOYMENT

Job discrimination contributes to doubling African American and Hispanic men's rates of unemployment compared to white men with the same level of education. In 1996, a time of almost full employment, the unemployment rate for both white men and women (age 20 and older) was 4.1 percent, while that of African-American women was 8.7 percent and that of African-American men was 9.4 percent (unpublished data, U.S. Bureau of Labor Statistics 1997). During recessions and for regions with depressed economies, the racial disparity is even greater (Moland 1996, p. 418). For example, in 1983, the year with the highest unemployment in recent memory, white men age 20 and older experienced a 7.9-percent unemployment rate, while the unemployment rates of same-age African-American men exceeded 18 percent. Very likely race differences exceed those reported above because African Americans

38

are more likely than whites to have given up on an active search for employment and hence are not counted in the unemployment rate (Lichter 1988). Not only are African Americans more likely than whites to be unemployed, it takes them longer than whites, on average, to find a job (Bureau of National Affairs 1995, pp. 5–38).

UNDEREMPLOYMENT

White women and racial minorities are more likely than white men to be underemployed—working part time because they cannot find full-time jobs or working full time for below-poverty-level wages—or out of the labor force (Lichter 1988). African-American men are twice as likely as white men to hold part-time jobs although they would prefer full-time employment, and African-American women and Hispanic men and women are two-and-a-half times more likely than are same-sex whites to work part time because a full-time job is not available (computed from U.S. Bureau of Labor Statistics 1995b).

Women are more likely than men to be trapped in marginal employment, and fully employed women are at greater risk than similar men of becoming underemployed. African-American women are more likely than non-African-American women to be underemployed (Lichter and Landry 1991, pp. 82–3). An expression of minorities' and women's greater risk of marginal employment is their overrepresentation in jobs that lack security. For example, African-American men are a third again as likely as white men and African-American women are about a fifth again as likely as white women to work in jobs of uncertain duration (Kalleberg et al. 1997; U.S. Bureau of Labor Statistics 1995a, tables 1–13). In general, women and minority men are more likely than white men to be employed in nonstandard work arrangements, even as professionals (Spalter-Roth et al. 1997).[19] Workers in these nonstandard jobs, on average, receive lower wages than do workers with similar personal characteristics and educational qualifications in regular full-time jobs (Kalleberg et al. 1997).

JOB ADVANCEMENT

Sex and race segregation in entry-level jobs, sex- and race-segregated career ladders (i.e., promotion ladders that link sex-segregated jobs), and discriminatory evaluation systems block the job advancement of people of color and white women (Baron, Davis-Blake, and Bielby 1986; Baldi and McBrier 1997). Discriminatory job assignments segregate female and minority workers into jobs that rarely lead to high-level positions in organizations (Bell and Nkomo 1994, p. 39). Male workers are 40 percent more likely than females to have been promoted by their current employer, net of education, experience, and other merit-based factors (Kalleberg and Reskin 1995; Erdreich et al. 1996, p. xi). This occurs partly because men are more likely to hold jobs that have regular procedures for promoting workers (Cassirer and Reskin 1998). Career ladders in the retail grocery industry are illustrative. Store managers are often recruited from the pool of produce managers who are drawn from the pool of produce clerks, a predominantly male job. In contrast, predominantly female jobs such as bakery clerk positions are dead-end or on short ladders (Reskin and Padavic 1994, p. 89). In large part, this reflects the short or nonexistent career ladders in jobs into which segregation concentrates women and minority men (Baron and Bielby 1985, pp. 238, 242; Baron, Davis-Blake, and Bielby 1986, p. 263; DiPrete 1989, p. 197; Collins 1993, 1997; Kalleberg and Reskin 1995).

Job segregation relegates women and minorities to jobs that are, on average, less complex than those that white men typically hold, and that are less likely to involve supervisory responsibility or decisionmaking authority (McGuire and Reskin 1993; Tomaskovic-Devey 1993). Since complex and challenging job assignments increase workers' chance of a promotion (Bell and Nkomo 1994, p. 39), segregating women and minorities into less challenging jobs decreases their chances of a promotion.

Jobs that are most likely to go to minorities and white women provide fewer opportunities than predominantly white-male jobs for workers to demonstrate their skills or to acquire new ones (Erdreich et al. 1996, p. xiii). For example, female managers have had fewer opportunities than male managers to resurrect a troubled business (Van Velsor and Hughes-James 1990), and male managers are more likely than female managers to hold jobs that involve high stakes and pressure from sources outside the organization (Ohlott et al. 1994, table 3). In addition, female and minority managers are disproportionately concentrated in EEO, human resources, and public relations, all staff functions and feminized and racialized roles that rarely lead to top management (Collins 1989, 1997; Bell and Nkomo 1994, pp. 32, 39; Durr and Logan 1997).

The higher the level of a job in an organization, the less permeable the barriers to mobility for sex- and race-atypical workers. In 1995, Fortune 1000 companies' employees were 46 percent female and 21 percent people of color, but 97 percent of the senior managers were white men. Women make up fewer than five percent of senior managers, and most female senior managers are white (Catalyst 1996; Dobrzynski 1996, p. C3). In general, African Americans, Asians, and Hispanics are well behind whites in reaching the vice-presidential level in corporations (Glass Ceiling Commission 1995).

EARNINGS

Sex and race segregation in the kinds of jobs workers hold and the establishments in which they work helps to produce pay gaps between white and African-American women and men. Because the firms in which women work pay less than those in which men work, the sexes'

41

segregation into different firms accounts for a substantial proportion of the earnings gap between the sexes (Carrington and Troske 1994, p. 530; 1998a). For example, one of the most comprehensive studies of the effect of sex segregation on the pay gap found that if women worked in the same occupations as men and in the same establishments, the pay gap would all but disappear (Petersen and Morgan 1995, p. 361).

The earnings disparities between the races and sexes among full-time workers in 1995 was considerable, although we do not know how much job segregation contributed to these disparities. The median annual earnings of African-American men and white women were 73 percent of those of white men; African-American women's were 63 percent; Hispanic men's were 62 percent; and Hispanic women's were 54 percent (computed from U.S. Bureau of Labor Statistics 1996, table 37). Economist Barbara Bergmann (1996, pp. 39–41) estimated that discrimination costs the average African-American male full-time worker at least $1,500 annually, and the average African-American or white woman about $3,400.

White men consistently out-earn women and minorities with equivalent years of education. These differences hold for all races: In 1989, for example, Asian-American professionals earned less than whites, despite more formal education (Harrison and Bennett 1995, p. 175). Particularly troubling is the fact that the wage gap between African Americans and whites has been widening, especially among college graduates. In 1979, African-American male college graduates earned 94 percent of what white men earned; in 1989, their share of white men's earnings had fallen to 86 percent (Carnoy and Rothstein 1996). In 1990, African-American men with professional degrees earned 21 percent less than their white counterparts in the same job categories (Shaw et al. 1993). Although African-American female graduates averaged slightly higher earnings than white female graduates in 1979, they earned eight

42

percent less in 1989. During this period, Latinos also lost ground relative to whites with the same levels of education (Carnoy and Rothstein 1996).

CONCLUSION

This chapter has shown that sex and race discrimination constrains minorities' and women's access to many jobs through employers' propensities and practices such as biased evaluation procedures, word-of-mouth hiring, and the requirement of unneeded credentials. Discrimination involves the interaction between individuals' actions and attitudes, and formal and informal organizational structures. These processes, "started by past events, now routinely bestow . . . advantages on white males and impose disadvantages . . . on minorities and women" (U.S. Commission on Civil Rights 1981, p. 13). Through discrimination, negative stereotyping, and organizational inertia, these practices— whether intentional or unintentional, formal or informal—are self perpetuating. Race and sex discrimination in recruitment, hiring, job assignment, and promotion segregate minorities and women into different jobs than those white men typically hold.

Sex and race segregation, in turn, restricts workers' access to job skills, promotions, authority, and earnings. Thus, through job segregation, discrimination leads to disparities in levels of employment, earnings, and opportunities to advance. By reducing job segregation that results from discrimination, affirmative action aims to narrow these unwarranted differences in access to and rewards from employment.

Chapter 3

THE EFFECTIVENESS OF AFFIRMATIVE ACTION IN COMBATTING JOB DISCRIMINATION

Employment discrimination is so thoroughly embedded in the ways firms do business that no single policy can eradicate it. Anti-discrimination laws have eliminated many blatant forms of discrimination. Nevertheless, discrimination remains common in America's workplaces, as was shown in Chapter 2. Even if every employer practiced affirmative action with the government's sustained and enthusiastic support, some race and sex discrimination would persist. Discrimination resides in people's unconscious attitudes as well as employers' long-standing practices, and it persists because human beings and organizations are creatures of habit. The further we depart from the hypothetical situation in which all employers enthusiastically practice affirmative action at the behest and with the support of government regulatory agencies, the more limited the impact of affirmative action.

Estimates in Chapter 1 indicate that only a small minority of U.S. employers are governed by affirmative action mandates. Many more practice affirmative action voluntarily, but there is even less reason to expect voluntary programs to reduce discrimination appreciably. Moreover, the Federal programs that require affirmative action demand relatively little of Federal contractors, rarely sanction recalcitrant em-

44

ployers, and have been enforced half-heartedly.[20] To overcome intentional discrimination, stereotyping, informal discriminatory practices, and organizational inertia, affirmative action would need to extend to all employers. The modest affirmative action activities that the presidential executive orders require of government employers and Federal contractors—assessing whether and why women and minorities are underrepresented and formalizing some human resource policies—precludes affirmative action substantially affecting the workforce as a whole. Thus, the overall impact of affirmative action as practiced in the United States to eradicate discrimination is limited. Nonetheless, this chapter shows that Federal affirmative action regulations—when implemented— have reduced discrimination. Court-ordered affirmative action and some voluntary programs have also been successful.

In theory, affirmative action policies and procedures should prevent discrimination by challenging ingrained patterns of racial and gender segregation in the workplace (Stephanopoulos and Edley 1995; Norton, 1996). How effective has affirmative action been in overcoming entrenched discriminatory practices? This chapter considers the research evidence on affirmative action's effects on Americans' access to equal employment opportunity. Most of this research compares firms that are subject to the OFCCP regulations with those that are not. Additional evidence on the effectiveness of affirmative action comes from comparing how minorities and women fared during periods when the OFFCP was enforcing the contract compliance program with times when it was not. Further evidence comes from comparing firms with affirmative action policies to those without such policies; case studies of firms, organizations, and industries; and declines in the level of occupational sex and race segregation over the past 30 years. Finally, this chapter reviews the research on whether affirmative action has negative consequences for its intended beneficiaries.

45

EFFECTS OF FEDERAL CONTRACT COMPLIANCE PROGRAMS

Comparisons of the workforce composition of Federal contractors covered by the OFCCP with noncontractors indicate that affirmative action has modestly improved minorities' and white women's access to jobs from which they had been excluded. We first examine research on the effects on minority men and women; then we consider research on the effects on white women.

Effects on Minority Men and Women

According to several studies, the employment of African-American workers by Federal contractors grew more rapidly during the 1970s than in firms that did not hold contracts with the Federal government (Badgett and Hartmann 1995). On average, African-American men's share of jobs increased almost one percent per year faster in contractor than noncontractor firms (Ashenfelter and Heckman 1976; Leonard 1984a, 1984b). Before 1974, minority employment in contractor firms grew primarily in unskilled and semi-skilled jobs (Ashenfelter and Heckman 1976; Heckman and Wolpin 1976; Leonard 1984b). Between 1974 and 1980, the contract compliance program and compliance reviews were associated with increases in African-American women's representation in all occupational categories except technical and crafts. African-American men at all skill levels benefited, although more skilled African-American men benefited most (Leonard 1984b). Thus, the effects of affirmative action have not been limited to skilled or highly educated minority workers (Graham 1992, p. 61; Hartmann 1996, p. 93).

Affirmative action has also enhanced other minorities' access to professional, managerial, and craft occupations (Leonard 1984b, p. 382). Organizations that became Federal contractors during the early 1980s (just before a precipitous drop in OFCCP funding) increased their share

46

of minority workers by 25 percent more than noncontractors did, and 20 percent more than did organizations that became contractors before 1980 (Edelman and Petterson 1993, p. 26). Relative to white men, affirmative action increased the occupational status on non-African-American minority males by two percent (Leonard 1994, p. 37). However, the positive contract-compliance effect observed for African Americans in 1992 did not hold for Hispanics, who remained underrepresented among Federal contractors relative to their share of the labor force (Rodgers and Spriggs 1996, p. 292).

Finally, at least one-third of the earnings gains among Latino and African-American men and women during the 1960s is attributable to declines in wage discrimination which are due jointly to anti-discrimination and affirmative action regulations (Carnoy 1994, p. 185).

Effects on White Women

Assessing the effect of affirmative action on white women's access to jobs traditionally closed to them is difficult because the period in which the government implemented affirmative action regulations coincided with the rapid increase in women's labor force participation. The flood of hundreds of thousands of women into the labor force increased women's share of jobs with both Federal contractors and noncontractors. For this reason, statistical studies of the effect of the contract compliance program on women yield mixed results. One study reported that contract compliance regulations improved women's access to customarily male occupations (Beller 1982). But others report that white women (as well as African-American women and men) were significantly less likely to hold white-collar jobs for Federal contractors than for noncontractors (Heckman and Wolpin 1976), and that in the late 1970s white men's occupational status at Federal contractors improved more rapidly than that of white women (Leonard 1984b, p. 384). These patterns vary over

47

time. For example, a contemporary survey of Philadelphia firms found that Federal contractors employed disproportionately more female managers than did firms without Federal contracts (Konrad and Linnehan 1995a). In general, however, the effect of the Federal contract compliance program on white women has been mixed (Leonard 1994, p. 37).

Comparing contractors' and noncontractors' workforces may over- or underestimate the impact of affirmative action. Such comparisons will overstate the effectiveness of affirmative action to the extent that Federal contractors attracted minority workers and women from jobs with noncontractors, thereby improving the job opportunities of some minority workers and women without reducing minorities' and women's aggregate disadvantage (Donohue and Heckman 1991). For this to have occurred, minority and female employees at firms without Federal contracts would have needed to know that contractors offered better jobs, to have applied for these jobs, and to have been hired. There is no evidence whether these three things occurred. On the other hand, comparing contractors' and noncontractors' workforces will understate affirmative action effects to the extent that affirmative action reduced discrimination by noncontractors, either by changing employment practices throughout the industry or through court orders against noncontractors.

In sum, although comparing contractors with noncontractors imperfectly estimates the impact of affirmative action, a preponderance of evidence indicates that the executive order, when enforced, helped to weaken discriminatory barriers to employment by Federal contractors for minorities (Leonard 1994, p. 35).

Studies Using Trend Data

As noted above, when the OFCCP was enforcing the contract compliance regulations during the 1970s, minorities were better represented among Federal contractors than noncontractors. During the early 1980s, when the OFCCP's mandate to enforce the Federal contract-compliance provisions and its budget were curtailed,[21] African Americans were better represented among noncontractors than contractors (Leonard 1994, p. 21). This finding suggests that when Federal contractors realized that the government was not enforcing the executive order, they reverted to their discriminatory business practices. In 1992, when the administration again supported affirmative action, Federal contractors were once again more likely than noncontractors to employ African-American men and women (Rodgers and Spriggs 1996, pp. 291–3).

EFFECTS AMONG GOVERNMENT WORKERS

In encouraging Federal agencies to take positive steps to ensure equal employment opportunity, Executive Orders 11246 (1965) and 11748 (1969) effectively instructed government employers to practice affirmative action. The 1972 Equal Employment Opportunity Act added the stamp of the law to the agencies' mandate to eliminate race and sex discrimination. These regulations lacked teeth, however. They did not provide for any sanctions, and the oversight agencies had no authority over the Federal agencies' efforts to prevent discrimination through affirmative action (Rosenbloom 1977; Stephanopoulos and Edley 1995).

Because the executive orders simultaneously barred discrimination of any kind based on factors not relevant to job performance (Executive Order 11748), it is impossible to separate the effects of anti-discrimination and affirmative-action provisions. Nonetheless, trend data show job integration that probably stemmed partly from the executive orders and the 1972 law requiring Federal agencies to take positive steps to eliminate discrimination. For example, between 1982 and 1995, Hispanics' share of Federal jobs increased by three percentage points, and African Americans' share increased by 1.6 percentage points (U.S. Bureau of the Census 1998). Importantly, women and minorities were also increasingly employed in higher-level jobs. In 1970, between two and four percent of female and African-American government employees were managers compared to 10 percent of white men (U.S. Bureau of the Census 1972, table 2). In 1990, however, 19 percent of white male Federal employees were managers, compared to 21 percent of white women, 17 percent of African-American women, and 13 percent of African-American men. Only African-American men did not narrow their gap with white men (computed from U.S. Bureau of the Census 1992).

Thus, affirmative action in the Federal government appears to have helped raise women's and male Hispanics' representation in middle-level administrative positions (DiPrete 1987). However, in the top grades (grades 13 to 15), minorities made less progress—1.5 percentage points for Hispanics and 2.9 percentage points for African Americans—because the growth in white employment (over 77 thousand jobs) swamped that of African Americans (14,000 new jobs) and Hispanics (6,500 new jobs; U.S. Bureau of the Census 1998). Rates of progress in Federal employment vary by agency,[22] reflecting agencies' autonomy in developing plans and their varying commitment to affirmative action.

During the same period, women's and minorities' share of state and local government jobs also grew. For example, African Americans' and Hispanics' shares each grew by five percentage points between 1973 and 1993, and women's job share increased by nine percentage points (U.S. Bureau of the Census 1998). While the earnings disparity between African Americans and non-Hispanic whites shrank by less than one percentage point during these 20 years, women's shortfall relative to men's median annual salaries narrowed by 6.5 percentage points, and Hispanics closed their gap with non-Hispanic whites by ten percentage points.

In sum, since the executive orders of Presidents Johnson and Nixon and the 1972 Equal Employment Opportunity Act required Federal agencies to pursue an "affirmative program of equal employment opportunities," minorities and women have become less segregated in Federal, state, and local government jobs, and Hispanics and women have narrowed their pay gaps with non-Hispanic white male government workers.

COMPARISONS OF AFFIRMATIVE-ACTION AND NONAFFIRMATIVE-ACTION EMPLOYERS

Quantitative and qualitative studies that compared firms with and without affirmative action procedures suggest positive outcomes of affirmative action for women and minorities. For example, recent surveys of employers in Los Angeles, Atlanta, Boston, and Detroit indicate that firms that reportedly considered affirmative action in hiring were ten percent more likely to have hired white women and 20 percent more likely to have hired African-American men than firms that did not practice affirmative action, net of other factors that affected hiring decisions (Holzer and Neumark 1998; Turner 1996, p. 22). There was, however, no effect for African American or Hispanic women (Holzer and Neumark 1998).

Studies of minorities' and women's representation across jobs in specific firms and industries also point to affirmative action's effectiveness in preventing employment discrimination. For example, women made considerable inroads into nontraditional jobs in industries that the OFCCP had targeted or in which leading firms were subject to court orders, including the banking and steel industries (Deaux and Ullman 1983; Reskin and Roos 1990; Blair-Loy 1996, p. 22). Also, women's representation among managers and officials in Cleveland's five largest banks climbed by more than 20 percent after the OFCCP reviewed the banks' employment practices in 1978 (U.S. Department of Labor 1996, p. 6).

The presidential executive order requiring affirmative action, along with pressure from the EEOC, precipitated sharp gains in African Americans' representation in South Carolina's textile industry (Heckman and Payner 1989). Xerox Corporation's voluntary affirmative action program increased minorities' share of jobs from three percent to 27 percent between 1964 and 1996 (Rand 1996). Affirmative-action seniority overrides in AT&T that stemmed from its 1972 consent decree with the EEOC reduced job segregation by sex by 14 percent in six years (Northrup and Larson 1979). Merck & Co., by treating its affirmative action efforts like any other business objective, increased women's representation among employees and among managers by five percentage points (Bureau of National Affairs 1986a, p. 124). During the same period, stimulated by a 1973 discrimination suit, General Motors's "aggressive affirmative action plan" increased women's and minorities' share of managerial jobs by four to five percentage points (Bureau of National Affairs 1986a, pp. 115–16). A discrimination suit also spurred the BankAmerica's affirmative action activities. Their results can be seen in minorities' and women's overrepresentation in management at BankAmerica relative to the industry. In 1985, minorities' and women's representation in managerial jobs at the bank exceeded industry averages by eight to 12 percentage points (Bureau of National Affairs 1986a, pp. 103–4).

Affirmative action was also instrumental in curtailing race and sex discrimination in public law enforcement. Between 1970 and 1990, the numbers of minority and female police officers in the U.S. increased tenfold: from less than 10,000 to 97,000 minorities and from less than 2,000 to more than 20,000 women (Bendick 1997). Both court-ordered and voluntary affirmative action plans led to less discriminatory hiring, but the effect of court-ordered plans was greater, presumably because such plans included goals and monitoring (Martin 1991, p. 495). During the 1970s and 1980s—a period during which courts ordered about 40 percent of police departments to engage in affirmative action because they had systematically discriminated against minorities and women in hiring, and another 42 percent of police departments adopted voluntary plans—minorities' representation among police officers shot up from seven percent to 22.5 percent, and women's share rose from two to nine percent (Martin 1991).

DECLINES IN OCCUPATIONAL SEGREGATION

Chapter 2 documented pervasive job segregation, reflecting minorities' and women's virtual exclusion from many lines of work. If affirmative action has curtailed the race and sex discrimination in access to jobs that gave rise to race and sex segregation, we should see declines in sex and race segregation over the last quarter century. Segregation indices for 1970, 1980, and 1990 capture changes in the levels of sex and race segregation during this period.[23] In 1970, the index of occupational segregation by sex was 67, indicating that about two-thirds of all women would have had to have changed occupations for the sexes to be similarly distributed across occupations. In 1980, the index was 60, and in 1990 it was 53. After 60 years of fluctuating between 65 and 70 (Gross 1968), the sex segregation index dropped by 20 percent in two decades. The index of occupational segregation for African Americans and whites dropped from 37 in 1970 to 29.5 in 1980, and 27 in 1990 (calculated from U.S. Bureau of the Census 1972, 1983, 1992).[24] This 27-percent decline in occupational segregation by race signals the inroads African Americans made into predominantly white occupations between 1970 and 1990.

Occupational desegregation opened to minorities and women desirable jobs from which they had been excluded. African-American men made particular gains in the skilled crafts. In 1960, one in ten held such jobs, compared with 20.9 percent of white men; by 1970, 15.4 percent of African-American men worked in skilled crafts, compared with 21.9 percent of whites (U.S. Bureau of the Census 1963, table 25, 1973, table

53

2).[25] African-American women made the greatest headway in clerical occupations.[26] In 1960, 7.4 percent held such jobs, compared with 26 percent in 1990 (U.S. Bureau of the Census 1963, table 3).[27] White women's greatest gains were in managerial and administrative jobs: 5.5 percent were managers and administrators in 1960; 27 percent were managers and administrators by 1990.[28] The proportions of African-American women and men in management rose from two and four percent, respectively, in 1970 and to 18.6 and 13.3 percent, respectively, in 1990 (U.S. Bureau of Labor Statistics 1971, 1991). Although many factors have contributed to women's and minorities' increased representation in these jobs, the findings summarized above suggests that, by preventing discrimination, affirmative action has opened thousands of jobs to women and minorities that discrimination had formerly closed to them.

Declining job segregation has helped to narrow the pay gap between white men and men and women of color. For example, in 1969 African-American women who worked full time year round earned only 46 percent of what white men earned; in 1996, they earned 60 percent as much (Browne 1998, table 1). African-American men averaged 70 percent of white men's earnings in 1969; by 1996 the disparity had narrowed to 75 percent. While significant wage disparities persist, the research evidence shows that they have narrowed.

ARE TARGETS OF AFFIRMATIVE ACTION ADVERSELY AFFECTED?

In assessing the effectiveness of affirmative action, we must consider whether it adversely affects its beneficiaries by fostering in them or their co-workers the belief that they are not qualified for their jobs (e.g., Steele 1990; O'Neill and O'Neill 1992, p. 103). In a society that subscribes to a meritocratic ideology, people may find it demeaning to get a job because of their sex or race. This section reviews research on whether affirmative action induces self-doubt in members of target groups and on whether others assume that the beneficiaries of affirmative action are unqualified.

Self-doubt by Targets

If benefiting from affirmative action leads women and minorities to doubt their abilities, then it defeats its objective of enhancing equal opportunity. According to Shelby Steele (1990), "The effect of preferential treatment—the lowering of normal standards to increase African-American representation—puts African Americans at war with an expanded realm of debilitating doubt, so that the doubt itself becomes an unrecognized preoccupation that undermines their ability to perform." What do the data show?

The beneficiaries of affirmative action should doubt their abilities only if (1) they believe that they obtained a position because of affirmative action, and (2) obtaining a position through affirmative action leads them to question their ability. Available research indicates that seven to eight percent of white women and 20 to 30 percent of African Americans think that they have benefited from affirmative action (Moore 1995; Hochschild 1995, p. 101; Molyneux 1996, p. 17; Verhovek 1997, p. 32).[29] Thus, while some minorities and women are potentially subject to self-doubt that results from believing affirmative action benefited them, most members of the targeted groups should be immune to this source of self-doubt because most do not think that affirmative action has helped them get a job or promotion.

According to laboratory experiments, only women who believe that they were selected for a leadership role entirely on the basis of their sex (almost no research has examined the effect of affirmative action based on race; Crocker and Major 1989; Kravitz et al. 1997, p. 34) suffer adverse psychological effects. Female college students who served as experimental subjects tended to devalue their abilities more when they were told that they were selected solely on the basis of their sex than when they were told that they were selected on the basis of merit (Heilman, Simon, and Repper 1987; Heilman, Block, and Lucas 1992; Heilman 1994; Turner et al. 1991; for a review, see Kravitz et al. 1997, pp. 33–5).[30] Female managers who believed that they had been promoted mainly because of their sex were less satisfied with their jobs than other women (Nacoste 1990). However, women who believe that sex as well as merit was among the criteria for their selection suffered no negative psychological effects (Major, Feinstein, and Crocker 1994, pp. 133–5; Turner and Pratkanis 1994, p. 63). Importantly, since OFCCP regulations and Supreme Court rulings insist that qualifications be the primary basis for selecting candidates, beneficiaries of affirmative action are selected primarily on the basis of merit.

Further evidence that benefiting from affirmative action does not have serious negative consequences comes from a comparison of the job attitudes of minorities and women whose employers engaged in affirmative action and those whose employers did not. African-American women, African-American men, and white women whose employers practiced some form of affirmative action were as satisfied with their jobs as their counterparts whose employers did not engage in affirmative action, according to a 1990 national survey of Americans (Taylor 1994b). This finding is consistent with the laboratory experiments cited above that showed no adverse effects of being chosen partly on the basis of merit as well as sex.

Stigmatization by Others

Both experimental studies in which undergraduate students are subjects and surveys of actual workers indicate that people often assume that

56

women and minorities who purportedly got their jobs because of affirmative action are less competent than other women and minorities. For example, managers who lacked information on a hypothetical female worker's performance rated women labeled as "affirmative action hires" as less competent than those not so labeled (Heilman et al. 1992, p. 541). These negative effects suggest that affirmative action and equal employment policies lead to the presumption that standards have been relaxed.

However, according to a 1995 Gallup poll, just eight percent of white women, 19 percent of African-American women, and 29 percent of African-American men have *ever* felt that their colleagues at work *or* school questioned their abilities or qualifications because of affirmative action (Crosby and Herzberger 1996, p. 62). In addition, although African-American male survey respondents employed in affirmative action firms described their evaluations as less positive than African-American men employed in nonaffirmative action firms, the opposite pattern held for African-American women (Taylor 1994b).

Thus, the data indicate that stigmatization by others is not widespread. Although some members of target groups feel stigmatized by affirmative action, they are in the minority, in part because few members of target groups think that affirmative action has affected them. For instance, a survey of female top executives revealed that 22 percent felt that affirmative action had both positive and negative effects on their careers, but just one percent felt that affirmative action's effects had been entirely negative (Catalyst 1996, p. 55).

Importantly, the tendency of some people to stigmatize members of groups targeted for affirmative action does not necessarily mean that affirmative action is the real cause of the stigmatization. Sex and race stereotypes in combination with the sex and race labeling of jobs foster a presumption that white men obtain customarily-male jobs because they are the most qualified, although, as we have seen, most obtain their jobs partly through personal contacts. The cultural devaluation of women and minorities seems to give these groups, but not white men, the burden of proving that they are qualified for jobs that white men usually perform.

In contexts in which discrimination continues to restrict minorities' and women's access to jobs and stereotypes cast doubt on their abilities, female and minority workers who challenge exclusionary practices may find themselves in a lose-lose situation: Either they are excluded because of discrimination with the attendant psychological and economic costs, or affirmative action prevents discriminatory exclusion but introduces the risk of stigmatization. Eliminating affirmative action would prevent the second kind of cost, while raising the likelihood of the first.[31] Fortunately, affirmative action employers can minimize the stigmatization of members of targeted groups by taking steps to ensure that all employees understand that qualifications are the primary consideration in all job assignments and promotions.

Other Effects on Members of Targeted Groups

By opening jobs to minorities and women from which they have been excluded, affirmative action allows them to acquire skills and experience that will enhance their productivity and add to the nation's stock of human capital. Moreover, the existence of affirmative action programs raises minorities' and women's aspirations. According to a large body of research, people's perceptions of opportunity affect their aspirations. Just as people respond to blocked opportunities by lowering their aspirations, they pursue opportunities that are open to them (Kanter 1977; Reskin and Hartmann 1986; Markham, Harlan, and Hackett 1987; Jacobs 1989; Cassirer and Reskin 1998). By convincing minorities and white women that employers will not discriminate against them, affirmative action encourages minorities and women to pursue jobs formerly closed to them (Pettigrew and Martin 1987, p. 51; Reskin and Roos 1990).

58

CONCLUSION

The research presented in this chapter indicates that, when implemented, affirmative action programs required by the presidential executive orders have reduced discriminatory barriers faced by minority and female workers. Even the modest effects of the contract compliance program are noteworthy in view of the sporadic and often perfunctory enforcement of the executive order by the OFCCP. Trend data on minorities' and women's representation in government are consistent with affirmative action's beneficial effects. More dramatic are the effects of court-ordered affirmative action in some firms and industries because of mandated goals and timetables, and the effects of some voluntary plans because of the commitment of top leaders.

People not targeted for affirmative action may stereotype members of target groups as less competent than people who were chosen for positions without benefit of affirmative action, if they believe that affirmative action means selecting workers solely on the basis of group membership. Employers can prevent this by providing clear evidence that selection is based primarily on qualifications. When employers let target group members know that they were selected primarily because of their qualifications, the latter do not appear to question their abilities. Available evidence indicates that self-stigmatization is a minor problem, and, although stigmatization by others is a risk, employers can mitigate it by providing information on how their affirmative action programs work.

Chapter 4

WHAT MAKES AFFIRMATIVE ACTION WORK?

The activities that organizations pursue in the name of affirmative action run the gamut from describing themselves as equal employment opportunity employers in recruitment materials to considering the affirmative action implications of every personnel decision they make (DiTomaso 1993; Badgett and Hartmann 1995; Konrad and Linnehan 1995a, p. 802). This variation reflects the different sources of affirmative action, the diffusion of affirmative action practices among noncontractors, and what employers believe is in their best interests. This chapter first addresses the practices that are particularly effective in reducing discriminatory barriers to workers' access to jobs. Effective practices by employers included commitment of the firm's top leaders, formalized personnel practices, established goals, and monitoring a firm's progress toward those goals. Second, the chapter considers the interplay of agency enforcement and economic conditions in making affirmative action work.

THE ENVIRONMENT OF AFFIRMATIVE ACTION

Federal Contractors

Federal contract compliance regulations do not mandate specific procedures that Federal contractors must follow. Instead, they offer broad guidelines regarding the kinds of personnel practices that comply with the spirit of the executive orders and give Federal contractors considerable leeway in designing compliance plans and affirmative action procedures (Dobbin et al. 1993). As we have seen, these procedures include innovative recruiting practices that reach underrepresented groups and formalized human resource practices (Edelman and Petterson 1993).

Voluntary Plans

Many of the affirmative action procedures in which employers voluntarily engage are standard personnel practices that are common in bureaucratic organizations. These practices, sometimes termed "internal labor markets," include formal job descriptions; promotion ladders that link jobs; salary classification systems; regular, objective performance evaluations; and formal grievance procedures (Edelman, Abraham, and Erlanger 1992; Dobbin et al. 1993; Sutton et al. 1994). In fact, Federal anti-discrimination and affirmative action regulations have contributed to firms' development of internal labor markets that govern job assignments and promotions (Dobbin et al. 1993). Because internal labor markets "depersonaliz[e] decisions about human resources" by assigning employees to jobs based on ability rather than on their sex, race, or whom they know, they help to thwart discrimination (Dobbin et al. 1993, p. 401).

Both voluntary affirmative action practices and those that are required under the presidential executive orders evolved through experimentation by human resource specialists. Typically, these specialists attend to the activities of regulatory and judicial agencies, while taking into account their financial implications for firms (Dobbin et al. 1988; Dobbin et al. 1993; Sutton et al. 1994). Effective practices tend to spread throughout industries (Edelman et al. 1991).

EFFECTIVE AFFIRMATIVE ACTION PRACTICES BY EMPLOYERS

Certain affirmative action practices demonstrably reduce discriminatory barriers to equal opportunity. For instance, a necessary first step is assessing the degree to which minorities and white women are represented across all jobs relative to their representation in the labor market. If workers' race or sex is associated with their chance of being hired, their job assignment, or their likelihood of promotion, effective affirmative action programs seek to identify specific employment practices that give rise to those associations. In response to a substantial imbalance, employers may modify employment practices, such as advertising job openings to a wider and more diverse pool of prospective employees; posting notices of nonentry-level jobs so that all employees can learn about them; requiring only those qualifications that workers need to perform a job; and using objective standards to hire, promote, and lay off workers.

Leadership

The commitment of an organization's top executives to eliminating discrimination is critical to effective affirmative action (Shaeffer and Lynton 1979; Bielby and Baron 1984; O'Farrell and Harlan 1984; Vernon-Gerstenfeld and Burke 1985, p. 60; Thomas 1990; Konrad and Linnehan 1995a). An organization whose leaders support affirmative action is likely to implement substantive programs, and—as we show below—substantive programs translate affirmative action policies into nondiscriminatory practices. Thus, personnel and affirmative action officers indicate that managerial support is particularly important for an effective affirmative action effort (Hitt and Keats 1984). By taking steps to ensure fairness for all workers, organizational leaders create broad support for affirmative action programs (Taylor 1995, p. 1407). In 1968, for example, the president of Xerox told his managers that the company's failure to hire enough minorities had contributed to urban unrest, and that henceforth company policy would require taking affirmative action to end discrimination. This public commitment paved the way for a very effective affirmative action program (DiTomaso 1993; Rand 1996, p. 67).[32]

Formalization

An essential part of affirmative action is the replacement of subjective and biased personnel practices with practices that treat all prospective and actual workers uniformly. Uniform treatment is typically achieved by formalizing previous personnel practices (Edelman 1992; Dobbin, Sutton, Meyer, and Scott 1993). Examples of formalized personnel practices include job postings, open recruitment methods, and standard-ized evaluations. To the extent that formalization reduces subjectivity and cronyism and thereby permits employers to draw on more diverse talent pools, it is a highly effective affirmative action practice.

Procedural Fairness

The ultimate goal of affirmative action is fair employment practices. Both the intended beneficiaries of affirmative action and workers not targeted by it stand to gain from fair personnel procedures.[33] Thus, in order for a firm's affirmative action program to succeed, it must develop personnel policies that are both fair and perceived by all employees to be fair (Edelman and Petterson 1993, p. 30). Affirmative action profession-als stress the importance of grievance procedures in fair personnel policies (Hitt and Keats 1984, p. 215). Educational efforts by employers are critical to generating support for fair procedures (Leonard 1994, p. 59) as well as to preventing the perception that affirmative action means hiring less qualified workers.

Organizational Structures and Substantive Programs

The existence of equal employment opportunity or affirmative action offices is associated with organizations engaging in affirmative action recruiting and training. These substantive programs, in turn, raise women's and minorities' representation. For example, firms with an affirmative action plan were eight times more likely than other firms to practice affirmative action in recruiting (Edelman and Petterson, 1993, p. 22).

Especially effective substantive structures treat race or gender as "plus factors" in decisions among qualified candidates for a job or promotion. These gender- and race-conscious affirmative action practices are associated with faster progress toward eliminating discriminatory barriers to women and lead to more equitable representation of minorities (Konrad and Linnehan 1995a).[34] As noted, the Supreme Court permits employers to implement race- and gender-conscious practices to remedy their past discrimination when they are narrowly tailored and do not unnecessarily deprive majority-group workers of jobs or promotions.

Goals and Monitoring

The sheer existence of goals seems to foster equity, regardless of whether an organization meets its goals (Leonard 1985). As several kinds of evidence attest, affirmative action is most effective in organizations that have goals for minorities' and women's representation across jobs. For example, a study of the link between Federal contractors' goals and minority employment during the 1970s showed that, while contractors' goals tended to be inflated, the size of a contractor's goal was the best predictor of how much progress minorities and women made in the contractor's workforce (Leonard 1990, p. 55). A more recent study of six affirmative action programs for women in construction revealed the same pattern: Although few projects met their goals, the higher the program's goals, the more women's representation improved (LeBreton, Loevy, and Sugerman 1995, p. 4). Further evidence of the importance of goals comes from a study of California state agencies cited by the State Personnel Board for sex and race discrimination. Although the Personnel Board imposed goals for only targeted jobs, it encouraged the agencies to integrate all jobs. However, only the targeted jobs became more integrated; the nontargeted jobs actually became more segregated (Baron, Mittman, and Newman 1991).

Having goals is most effective when organizations monitor their progress toward achieving those goals. Systematically monitoring progress toward goals is the essence of good business practice, whether the goal is increasing sales, reducing turnover, or eliminating discriminatory barriers to women and minorities. The importance of goals and monitoring systems is evident in comparisons of minority occupational integration in firms with Federal contracts during the 1970s, when the OFCCP required Federal contractors to set goals, with the 1980s, when the OFCCP did not require goals. Without numerical goals, employers were less likely to eliminate the discriminatory practices that suppressed minorities' representation across jobs (Leonard 1994). The U.S. Army's success in reducing race and sex disparities in promotion was due partly to its having set goals based on the pool of qualified female and minority candidates and then monitoring progress toward achieving those goals (Moskos 1996, pp. 228, 235).

Sanctions

Positive and negative sanctions provide powerful incentives for organizations to alter their behavior because incentive structures affect managers' performance. This means that affirmative action programs that are most effective in curtailing discrimination mandate substantive results (Edelman and Petterson 1993, p. 30) and evaluate and reward managers on their success in achieving those results (Vernon-Gerstenfeld and Burke 1985, p. 59; Bureau of National Affairs 1986a). Thus, the California State Personnel Board's threat to withhold resources from state agencies whose job assignments were extremely segregated led the targeted jobs to become more integrated (Baron et al. 1991).

Affirmative action sometimes involves personnel practices that reduce the discriminatory effects of managers' stereotypes on their decisions regarding job assignment and promotions. The effects of stereotypes and bias are reduced when decision makers know that they will be held accountable for the criteria they use to make decisions, the accuracy of the information upon which the decisions are based, and the consequences of their actions on equal employment opportunity (Salancik and Pfeffer 1978; Tetlock 1985, 1992; Pettigrew and Martin 1987; Tetlock and Kim 1987; Konrad and Linnehan 1995a; Eberhardt and Fiske 1996). Thus, by evaluating and rewarding managers on the basis of their affirmative action performance, establishments effectively suppress discrimination (Vernon-Gerstenfeld and Burke 1985, p. 59; Bureau of National Affairs 1986a).

EFFECTIVE AFFIRMATIVE ACTION PRACTICES BY ENFORCEMENT AGENCIES

The actions that regulatory agencies and the judiciary take to enforce anti-discrimination laws and affirmative action regulations influence the effectiveness of affirmative action plans in reducing race and sex discrimination. The Federal contract compliance program has been effective in surmounting inertia in employer's customary practices because being subject to OFCCP review prompts human resources and legal personnel to develop effective programs. Without pressure from regulatory agencies, affirmative action policies and affirmative action offices often fail to deter discrimination (Baron 1991, p. 134). As noted above, it took reprimands and the threat of budgetary sanctions by the California State Personnel Board to reduce sex and race segregation in California state agencies (Baron et al. 1991).

The activities of regulatory agencies and the courts send signals to employers regarding what forms of employment discrimination will be tolerated. Broad Federal policy affects firms' specific procedures as human resource personnel interact with OFCCP staff and react to judicial outcomes. In this way, the activities of regulatory agencies indirectly influence personnel practices in firms that are *not* covered by affirmative action regulations or anti-discrimination statutes, because human resources and legal staff in those firms attend to the activities of regulatory agencies and because their networks tend to include human resource and legal personnel in firms that are subject to regulations.

When enforcement agencies lack the mandate to pursue their agenda, this process of indirect influence in standard setting is aborted, and firms' employment practices shift in response to other priorities (Bergmann 1996). For example, Bureau of National Affairs' 1976 and 1985 surveys of 206 Fortune-500 firms show declines in several affirmative action practices. Most striking are the 20 percentage-point drop in targeted recruiting and the 15 percentage-point drop in promotion training for minorities (Kelly and Dobbin 1998, Figure 4). Surveys by the Bureau of National Affairs show slight declines in minority and female representation in Fortune-500 firms by the middle 1980s (1986b, p. 22). The reduction in effective affirmative action practices that followed the erosion of political support for affirmative action during the Reagan administration apparently had the predictable effect of reducing women's and minorities' access to jobs. Modifying personnel policies is more likely to precipitate genuine change when enforcement agencies have mandated the modifications (Deaux and Ullman 1983; Martin 1991). Therefore, enforcement activities by regulatory agencies are an important part of the process through which firms develop affirmative action procedures that effectively reduce discrimination.

Monitoring

A major limitation of anti-discrimination regulations is that they leave monitoring up to the victims of discrimination. Although thousands of people who have suffered discrimination have filed complaints or brought suit, most victims of discrimination do not do so (Donohue and Siegelman 1991, p. 1005), either because they do not know that discrimination cost them a job or promotion, or because they are too vulnerable to sue (only ten percent of discrimination complaints brought by nongovernment employees are against the complainants' current employer; Donohue and Siegelman 1991, p. 1031). Affirmative action mandated by executive order or judicial decree does not require actual or potential victims to monitor employers' compliance with the law. Instead, it assigns that responsibility to regulatory agencies that—given administration support—are better equipped for it.

The OFCCP monitors contractors covered by the executive order through compliance reviews that audit the race and sex composition of an establishment's jobs and investigate its personnel procedures. These routine audits uncover race and sex discrimination. In fact, the effect of a compliance review is more than twice that of being subject to the executive order (Leonard 1990, p. 51).

Sanctions

External sanctions provide powerful incentives for organizations to alter their behavior. The OFCCP's affirmative action program has been most effective when contractors not in compliance face a genuine risk of being sanctioned. Thus, although the number of compliance reviews by the OFCCP increased during the 1980s, their impact declined because the Reagan administration did not support sanctions (Leonard 1987;

1994, p. 10). Although the sanction of debarment has been invoked so rarely that few contractors probably view it as a genuine threat,[35] the lack of sanctions associated with purely voluntary efforts make them less effective than mandatory programs.[36]

ECONOMIC CONDITIONS

A healthy economy offers the best chances for enhancing equal opportunity. Affirmative action has been more effective among Federal contractors under favorable than unfavorable economic conditions (Leonard 1984a). An expanding number of jobs minimizes the likelihood that nontargeted groups will see affirmative action as a threat (Reskin and Roos 1990; Quillian 1995). By the same token, economic stagnation or even economic uncertainty puts affirmative action gains at risk for several clear reasons: (1) Women and minorities are overrepresented in staff positions like affirmative action and EEO posts that are easy targets for budget cutting (Collins 1997; Durr and Logan 1997); (2) workers who are not covered by affirmative action programs are less threatened by affirmative action during times of prosperity; and (3) a healthy economy allows employers to devote more attention and resources to issues that do not immediately affect the bottom line.

CONCLUSION

The practices that Federal contractors and noncontractors have adopted in the spirit of affirmative action vary, as the OFCCP guidelines recognized they would. Despite our limited knowledge regarding the prevalence of various affirmative action practices, we know a good deal about the kinds of affirmative action practices that are most effective.

Especially important for affirmative action to be effective is the moral and organizational authority of organizations' leaders. The formalization of personnel practices to incorporate procedural fairness for all workers

69

is a key mechanism of affirmative action. The sheer existence of goals enhances the success of affirmative action efforts, but goals are more effective when organizations regularly review their progress toward achieving them, when there is external pressure and standard setting by regulatory agencies to achieve results, and when internal and external sanctions exist.

Forces outside of establishments that help surmount the barriers of discrimination include direct activities and indirect influence of Federal agencies. Also significant are a healthy economy and educational programs that ensure that minorities and women are well represented among the pool of qualified candidates for available jobs.

Chapter 5

THE EFFECTS OF AFFIRMATIVE ACTION ON OTHER STAKEHOLDERS

Affirmative action policies and practices reduce job discrimination against minorities and white women, although their effects have not been large. Some critics charge that affirmative action's positive effects have been offset by its negative effects on white men, on productivity, and on the merit system. The research examined in this chapter shows that affirmative action rarely entails reverse discrimination, and neither hampers business productivity nor unduly increases the costs of doing business. Both theoretical and empirical research suggest that it enhances productivity by encouraging employment practices that better utilize workers' skills.

REVERSE DISCRIMINATION

For many people, the most troubling aspect of affirmative action is that it may discriminate against majority-group members (Lynch 1997). According to 1994 surveys, 70 to 80 percent of whites believed that affirmative action sometimes discriminates against whites (Steeh and Krysan 1996, p. 139). Men are more likely to believe that a woman will get a job or promotion over an equally or more qualified man than they are to believe that a man will get a promotion over an equally or more qualified women (Davis and Smith 1996). In short, many whites,

71

especially white men, feel that they are vulnerable to reverse discrimination (Bobo and Kluegel 1993). When asked whether African Americans or whites were at greater risk of discrimination at work, respondents named whites over African Americans by a margin of two to one (Steeh and Krysan 1996, p. 140). In addition, 39 percent of respondents to a 1997 *New York Times*/CBS News poll said that whites losing out because of affirmative action was a bigger problem than African Americans losing out because of discrimination (Verhovek 1997, p. 32).

Several kinds of evidence indicate that whites' fears of reverse discrimination are exaggerated. Reverse discrimination is rare both in absolute terms and relative to conventional discrimination.[37] The most direct evidence for this conclusion comes from the employment-audit studies described earlier: On every measured outcome, African-American men were much more likely than white men to experience discrimination, and Latinos were more likely than non-Hispanic men to experience discrimination (Heckman and Siegelman 1993, p. 218). Statistics on the numbers and outcomes of complaints of employment discrimination also suggest that reverse discrimination is rare.

According to national surveys, relatively few whites have experienced reverse discrimination. Only five to 12 percent of whites believe that their race has cost them a job or a promotion, compared to 36 percent of African Americans (Steeh and Krysan 1996, pp. 139–40). Of 4,025 Los Angeles workers, 45 percent of African Americans and 16 percent of Latinos said that they had been refused a job because of their race, and 16 percent of African Americans and eight percent of Latinos reported that they had been discriminated against in terms of pay or a promotion (Bobo and Suh 1996, table 1). In contrast, of the 863 whites surveyed, less than three percent had ever experienced discrimination in pay or promotion, and only one mentioned reverse discrimination. Nonetheless, two-thirds to four-fifths of whites (but just one-quarter of African

Americans) surveyed in the 1990s thought it likely that less qualified African Americans won jobs or promotions over more qualified whites (Taylor 1994a; Davis and Smith 1994; Steeh and Krysan 1996, p. 139).[38]

Alfred Blumrosen's (1996, pp. 5–6) exhaustive review of discrimination complaints filed with the Equal Employment Opportunity Commission offers additional evidence that reverse discrimination is rare. Of the 451,442 discrimination complaints filed with the EEOC between 1987 and 1994, only four percent charged reverse discrimination (see also Norton 1996, pp. 44–5).[39] Of the 2,189 discrimination cases that Federal appellate courts decided between 1965 and 1985, less than five percent charged employers with reverse discrimination (Burstein 1991, p. 518).

Statistics on the more than 3,000 cases that reached district and appeals courts between 1990 and 1994 show an even lower incidence of reverse discrimination charges: Less than two percent charged reverse discrimination (U.S. Department of Labor, Employment Standards Administration n.d. (b), p. 3). The small number of reverse-discrimination complaints by white men does not appear to stem from their reluctance to file complaints: They filed more than 80 percent of the age discrimination complaints that the EEOC received in 1994. Instead, as former EEOC chair Eleanor Holmes Norton (1996, p. 45) suggested, white men presumably complain most about the kind of discrimination that they experience most and least about discrimination they rarely encounter.

Allegations of reverse discrimination are less likely than conventional discrimination cases to be supported by evidence. Of the approximately 7,000 reverse discrimination complaints filed with the EEOC in 1994, the EEOC found only 28 credible (Crosby and Herzberger 1996, p. 55). Indeed, U.S. district and appellate courts dismissed almost all the reverse-discrimination cases they heard between 1990 and 1994 as lacking merit.

73

Although rare, reverse discrimination does occur. District and appellate courts found seven employers guilty of reverse discrimination in the early 1990s (all involved voluntary affirmative action programs), and a few Federal contractors have engaged in reverse discrimination, according to the OFCCP's director for Region II (Stephanopoulos and Edley 1995, Section 6.3).[40]

The actions and reports of Federal contractors are inconsistent with the belief that goals are *de facto* quotas that lead inevitably to reverse discrimination. In the first place, the fact that contractors rarely meet their goals means that they do not view them as quotas (Leonard 1990, p. 56). Second, only two percent of 641 Federal contractors the OFCCP surveyed in 1994 complained that the agency required quotas or reverse discrimination (Stephanopoulos and Edley 1995, Section 6.3).

How can we reconcile the enormous gulf between whites' perceptions that they are likely to lose jobs or promotions because of affirmative action and the small risk of this happening? The white men who brought reverse-discrimination suits presumably concluded that their employers' choices of women or minorities could not have been based on merit, because men are accustomed to being selected for customarily-male jobs (*New York Times*, March 31, 1995).[41] Most majority-group members who have not had a first-hand experience of competing unsuccessfully with a minority man or woman or a white woman cite media reports as the source of their impression that affirmative action prompts employers to favor minorities and women (Hochschild 1995, pp. 144, 308).[42] It seems likely that politicians' and the media's emphasis on "quotas" has distorted the public's understanding of what is required and permitted in the name of affirmative action (Entman 1997). It is also likely that the public does not distinguish affirmative action in employment from affirmative action in education which may include preferences or in the awarding of contracts which have included set-asides.

AFFIRMATIVE ACTION AND AMERICAN COMMERCE

Does affirmative action curb productivity, as some critics have charged? On the one hand, affirmative action could impede productivity if it forces employers to hire or promote marginally qualified and unqualified workers, or if the paperwork associated with affirmative action programs is burdensome. On the other hand, employers who assign workers to jobs based on their qualifications rather than their sex or race should make more efficient use of workers' abilities and hence should be more productive than those who use discriminatory employment practices (Becker 1971; Leonard 1984c; Donohue 1986). Affirmative action could also increase profitability by introducing varied points of view or helping firms broaden their markets (Cox and Blake 1991; Watson, Kumar, Michaelsen 1993).

Effects on Productivity

There is no evidence that affirmative action reduces productivity or that workers hired under affirmative action are less qualified than other workers. In the first place, affirmative action plans that compromise valid educational and job requirements are illegal. Hiring unqualified workers or choosing a less qualified person over a more qualified one because of their race or sex is illegal and is not condoned in the name of affirmative action (U.S. Department of Labor, Employment Standards Administration n.d. (b), p. 2). Second, to the extent that affirmative action gives women and minority men access to jobs that more fully exploit their productive capacity, their productivity and that of their employers should increase.

Although many Americans believe that affirmative action means that less qualified persons are hired and promoted (Verhovek 1997, p. 32), the evidence does not bear this out. According to a study of more than 3,000 workers hired in entry-level jobs in a cross-section of firms in

75

Atlanta, Boston, Detroit, and Los Angeles, the performance evaluations of women and minorities hired under affirmative action did not differ from those of white men or female or minority workers for whom affirmative action played no role in hiring (Holzer and Neumark 1998). In addition, Columbus, Ohio female and minority police officers hired under an affirmative action consent decree performed as well as white men (Kern 1996). Of nearly 300 corporate executives surveyed in 1979, 72 percent believed that minority hiring did not impair productivity (*Wall Street Journal* 1979); 41 percent of CEOs surveyed in 1995 said affirmative action improved corporate productivity (Crosby and Herzberger 1996, p. 86).[43]

Of the handful of studies that address the effect of affirmative action on productivity, none suggests a negative effect of the employment of women or minorities on productivity. First, the increasing representation of female and minority male workers between 1966 and 1977 and between 1984 and 1988 did not affect firms' productivity (Leonard 1984c; Conrad 1995). Second, in the context of policing, the proportions of minority or female officers are unrelated to measures of departments' effectiveness (Lovrich, Steel, and Hood 1986, p. 70; Steel and Lovrich 1987, p. 67). Third, according to a sophisticated analysis of 1990 data on establishments' and workers' characteristics, there is no relationship between firms' employment of women and their productivity in smaller plants, but in plants with more market power (and hence the capacity to discriminate), the more women plants employed, the better the firms' performance (Hellerstein, Neumark, and Troske 1998).

Studies assessing the effect of firms' racial makeup on their profits also show no effects of affirmative action on productivity. An analysis of 100 of Chicago's largest firms over a 13-year period found no statistically significant relationship between the firms' share of minority workers and their profit margins or return on equity (McMillen 1995).

76

This absence of an association is inconsistent with companies using lower standards when hiring African American employees. Finally, according to a study that compared the market performance of the 100 firms with best and worst records of hiring and promoting women and minorities, the former averaged an 18-percent return on investments, whereas the latter's average returns were below eight percent (Glass Ceiling Commission 1995, pp. 14, 61).[44]

Costs to Business

Estimates of the price tag of affirmative action range from a low of hundreds of millions of dollars to a high of $26 billion (Brimelow and Spencer 1993).[45] More realistic estimates put enforcement and compliance costs at about $1.9 billion (Leonard 1994, p. 34; Conrad 1995, pp. 37–8). According to Andrew Brimmer (1995, p. 12), former Governor of the Federal Reserve Board, the inefficient use of African Americans' productive capacity (as indicated by their education, training, and experience) costs the economy 70 times this much: About $138 billion annually which is about 2.15 percent of the gross national product. Adding the cost of sex discrimination against white women would substantially increase the estimated cost of discrimination because white women outnumber African American men and women in the labor force by about three to one. The more affirmative action reduces race and sex discrimination, the lower its costs relative to the savings it engenders.

The affirmative action that the Federal executive order requires of Federal contractors adds to their paperwork. Companies with at least $50,000 in Federal contracts that employ at least 50 employees must provide written affirmative action plans that include goals and timetables, based on an annual analysis of their utilization of their labor pool. They must also provide specified information to the OFFCP and keep detailed records on the composition of their jobs and job applicants by

77

race and sex. In response to an OFCCP survey soliciting their criticisms of the program, about one in eight Federal contractors complained about the paperwork burden (Stephanopoulos and Edley 1995, section 6.3). Keeping the records required by the OFCCP encourages the bureaucratization of human resource practices. As noted, informal employment practices, while cheaper in the short run, are also more subject to discriminatory bias and hence cost firms efficiency. Thus, implicit in the logic of the OFCCP's requirements is the recognition that formalizing personnel practices helps to reduce discrimination.

Business Support

U.S. business has supported affirmative action for at least 15 years. The Reagan administration's efforts to curtail the contract compliance program in the early 1980s drew strong opposition from the corporate sector (Bureau of National Affairs 1986a). Among the groups that went on record as opposing cutbacks in Federal affirmative action programs was the National Association of Manufacturers, a major organization of U.S. employers (*The San Diego Union-Tribune* 1985, p. AA-2). All but six of 128 heads of major corporations indicated that they would retain their affirmative action plans if the Federal government ended affirmation action (Noble 1986, p. B4). A 1996 survey showed similar levels of corporate support for affirmative action: 94 percent of CEOs surveyed said that affirmative action had improved their hiring procedures, 53 percent said it had improved marketing, and—as noted above—41 percent said it had improved productivity (Crosby and Herzberger 1996, p. 86). The business community's favorable stance toward affirmative action is also seen in the jump in stock prices for firms recognized by the OFCCP for their effective affirmative action programs (Wright et al. 1995, p. 281).

Perhaps the most telling sign of business support for affirmative action is the diffusion of affirmative action practices from Federal contractors to noncontractors. As noncontractors have recognized the efficiency or market payoffs associated with more objective employment practices and a more diverse workforce, many have voluntarily implemented some affirmative action practices (Fisher 1985).

AFFIRMATIVE ACTION AND OTHER STAKEHOLDERS

The consequences of affirmative action reach beyond workers and employers by increasing the pools of skilled minority and female workers. When affirmative action prompts employers to hire minorities or women for positions that serve the public, it can bring services to communities that would otherwise be underserved. For example, African-American and Hispanic physicians are more likely than whites and Anglos to practice in minority communities (Komaromy et al. 1996). Graduates of the Medical School at the University of California at San Diego who were admitted under a special admissions program were more likely to serve inner-city and rural communities and saw more poor patients than those admitted under the regular procedures (Penn, Russell, and Simon 1986).

Women's and minorities' employment in nontraditional jobs also raises the aspirations of other members of excluded groups by providing role models and by signaling that jobs are open to them. Some minorities and women do not pursue jobs or promotions because they expect to encounter discrimination (Mayhew 1968, p. 313). By reducing the perception that discriminatory barriers block access to certain lines of work, affirmative action curtails this self selection (Reskin and Roos 1990, p. 305). In addition, the economic gains provided by better jobs permit beneficiaries to invest in the education of the next generation.

AFFIRMATIVE ACTION, MERITOCRACY, AND FAIRNESS

Affirmative action troubles some Americans for the same reasons discrimination does: They see it as unfair and inconsistent with meritocracy (Nacoste 1990). The evidence summarized above indicates that employers very rarely use quotas and that affirmative action does not lead to the employment of unqualified workers. We know too that many employers implement affirmative action by expanding their recruiting efforts, by providing additional training, and by formalizing human resource practices to eliminate bias. By eliminating cronyism, drawing on wider talent pools, and providing for due-process, these practices are fairer to all workers than conventional business practices (*Harvard Law Review* 1989, pp. 668–70; Dobbin et al. 1993, pp. 401–6). After all, managers who judge minority and female workers by their race or sex instead of their performance may judge white workers by arbitrary standards as well (Rand 1996, p. 72).

Available research does not address how often employers take into account race and gender in choosing among equally qualified applicants. Although the courts have forbidden race- and gender-conscious practices in layoffs, they have allowed employers to take into account race or gender in selecting among qualified applicants in order to remedy the consequences of having previously excluded certain groups from some jobs. Such programs trouble some Americans, as we can see from the research evidence presented in the next section.

AMERICANS' VIEWS OF AFFIRMATIVE ACTION

The passage of the 1996 California Civil Rights Initiative, which barred this state from engaging in affirmative action, has been interpreted as signaling mounting public opposition to affirmative action. In reality, whites' and African Americans' views of affirmative action are both more nuanced and more positive than the California election result suggests. People's responses to opinion polls depend largely on how pollsters characterize affirmative action (Kravitz et al. 1997).[46] About 70 percent of Americans support affirmative action programs that pollsters describe as not involving "quotas" or "preferences" (Steeh and Krysan 1996, pp. 132, 134; Entman 1997, p. 37). Like a red flag, the term "quota" also triggers strong negative reactions. This happens because people view quotas as inconsistent with merit-based hiring and because quotas provoke fear of unfairly losing a job or promotion by members of groups that are not covered by affirmative action. As a result, most whites and African Americans oppose quotas (Bobo and Kluegel, 1993; Steeh and Krysan 1996, pp. 132–3, 148).

A casual reading of newspaper reports indicates considerable instability in Americans' attitudes toward affirmative action and a fair amount of opposition to affirmative action. For example, fewer than one in eight Americans surveyed in a 1995 Gallup poll approved of affirmative action programs that involve hiring quotas, and only 40 to 50 percent of Americans endorsed affirmative action programs designed to give African Americans or women preferential treatment (Moore 1995). However, polls that show low levels of support for affirmative action in the workplace typically ask about practices that are illegal and hence rare in actual affirmative action programs (Kravitz et al. 1997, p. xi). When pollsters ask about affirmative action in general or about the practices that actual affirmative action programs include, the majority of whites and African Americans are supportive.

In national polls conducted in the mid-1990s, about 70 percent of respondents endorsed affirmative action either as currently practiced or with reforms (Entman 1997, p. 37). For example, almost three-quarters of the respondents to a 1995 Gallup poll approved of employers using outreach efforts to recruit qualified minorities and women (Steeh and

Krysan 1996, pp. 132, 134). Most whites and African Americans support such practices as targeted recruitment, open advertising, monitoring diversity, job training, and educational assistance designed to allow minorities to compete as individuals (e.g., training programs). More than three out of four white respondents and 85 percent of African-American respondents to a 1991 Harris Survey agreed that "as long as there are no rigid quotas, it makes sense to give special training and advice to women and minorities so that they can perform better on the job" (Bobo and Kluegel 1993; Bruno 1995, p. 24).

We do not know how Americans feel about the kinds of race- or gender-conscious affirmative action that EEOC guidelines and Supreme Court rulings allow. When asked about "preferential hiring," most Americans disapprove. For example, only one-sixth to one-fifth of respondents surveyed during the 1990s favored the preferential hiring and promotion of African Americans because of past discrimination (about 10 to 17 percent of whites and about half to three-quarters of African Americans; Steeh and Krysan 1996, pp. 146–7). Just one survey phrased the question so that it approximately corresponded to what race- and gender-conscious affirmative action entails: giving a preference to a woman or minority over an equally qualified white man. Three quarters of respondents did not view this practice as discriminatory (Roper Center for Public Opinion 1995).

Overall, the public is less concerned with affirmative action than media accounts would have us believe (Entman 1997). For example, respondents to a 1996 *Wall Street Journal*/NBC News poll ranked affirmative action second to last in importance out of 16 issues.[47] As Robert Entman (1997) argued, the media's framing of affirmative action as controversial exaggerates white opposition to and public discord over it.

In sum, the polls reveal that the majority of whites and African Americans have supported affirmative action since the early 1970s. Most

Americans support the affirmative action procedures that employers actually use, such as taking extra efforts to find and recruit minorities and women. The broadest support is for practices that expand the applicant pool, but ignore race or gender in the selection process. Thus, Americans' first choice is enhancing equal opportunity without using race- or gender-conscious mechanisms. What most Americans oppose is quotas, an employment remedy that courts impose only under exceptional circumstances. Thus, the kinds of affirmative action practices most Americans support are in synch with what most affirmative action employers do.

CONCLUSION

Some critics charge that any positive effects of affirmative action come at too high a price. However, the evidence suggests that the predominant effects of affirmative action on American enterprise are neutral, and some are positive. Contrary to popular opinion, reverse discrimination is rare. Workers for whom affirmative action was a hiring consideration are no less productive than other workers. There is no evidence that affirmative action impairs productivity, and there is some evidence that, when properly implemented, affirmative action increases firms' efficiency by rationalizing their business practices. These neutral to positive effects of affirmative action contribute to the broad support it enjoys in corporate America. The affirmative action practices that appear to be most common—such as special training programs or efforts to expand recruitment pools (Bureau of National Affairs 1986a)—have the support of the majority of whites and people of color.

Although most affirmative action practices are neutral with respect to race and gender (e.g., eliminating subjectivity from evaluation systems), some employers take into account race and sex as "plus factors" in choosing among qualified candidates in order to reduce imbalances stemming from their past employment practices. Race- and gender-conscious practices are legal if they are part of court-ordered or voluntary affirmative action programs designed to correct a serious imbalance resulting from past exclusionary practices and as long as they are properly structured so that they do not unnecessarily or permanently limit the opportunities of groups not protected under affirmative action. At least one in four Americans oppose such race- and gender-conscious practices. More generally, any departure from strict reliance on merit troubles some Americans. Others favor taking into account group membership in order to eradicate America's occupational caste system, enhance equal opportunity, and strengthen the U.S. democracy (Steinberg 1995).

The tension between affirmative action and merit is the inevitable result of the conflict between our national values and what actually occurs in the nation's workplaces. As long as discrimination is more pervasive than affirmative action, it is the real threat to meritocracy. But because no one will join the debate on behalf of discrimination, we end up with the illusion of a struggle between affirmative action and merit.

Chapter 6

CONCLUSION AND POLICY IMPLICATIONS

This book has drawn on sociological, psychological, and economic research on affirmative action to address to five questions: (1) What is affirmative action in the employment context? (2) Does ongoing discrimination necessitate affirmative action? (3) Has affirmative action reduced sex and race discrimination? (4) What affirmative action practices are most effective in curtailing job and promotion discrimination? (5) How does affirmative action affect persons whom it does not target, employers, and society?

WHAT IS AFFIRMATIVE ACTION IN THE EMPLOYMENT CONTEXT?

Affirmative action in employment includes policies and procedures designed to prevent discrimination in the workplace and to rectify the continuing effects of present and past discrimination. Like anti-discrimination laws, the object of affirmative action is to make equal opportunity in the workforce a reality. Unlike anti-discrimination laws, which provide remedies to which workers can appeal after they have suffered discrimination, affirmative action policies attempt to prevent discrimination from occurring.

The policies and practices that affirmative action comprises grew out of presidential executive orders, litigation over discrimination charges, and employers' voluntary efforts as well as the requirements of regulatory

85

agencies. In pursuit of affirmative action, employers have formalized personnel practices such as job postings, evaluations, and grievance procedures; developed innovative recruitment strategies; instituted job training; and, under some conditions, treated gender or race as plus factors in choosing among qualified candidates. The nature of employers' affirmative action policies and practices depends, in part, on the reason they exist. Many affirmative action employers—many government agencies and about three percent of all private firms—have enacted policies and practices because they are bound to do so under executive orders that required Federal contractors and government employees to take positive steps to prevent discrimination against minorities and women.

Some establishments engage in affirmative action because Federal judges have ordered them to do so after finding them guilty of discrimination or they have agreed to do so in consent decrees resolving a discrimination suit. Court-ordered affirmative action differs from that required of Federal contractors because, under certain conditions, judges can mandate filling particular jobs with a specified number or proportion of minorities or women.

A substantial number of firms that are not required by executive orders or the courts to engage in affirmative action do so. Their affirmative actions may range from describing themselves as affirmative action employers to creating programs to recruit and train members of underrepresented groups. The Supreme Court has permitted a few employers to reserve some jobs for qualified members of protected groups when past discrimination has virtually excluded them from those jobs.

Anti-discrimination laws bar employers from giving preference to any group, except those that are under court order or are voluntarily pursuing activities to remedy long-standing discriminatory practices under conditions that protect the opportunities of whites and men. Thus, by and large, affirmative action refers to proactive employment practices whose object is to safeguard against job discrimination.

DOES ONGOING DISCRIMINATION WARRANT AFFIRMATIVE ACTION?

Although employment discrimination has declined over the last 40 years, it still persists both because employers consciously act on race and sex preferences in filling jobs and because many employment practices disadvantage minorities and white women. Some employers who do not willfully pursue discriminatory personnel practices do so inadvertently in carrying on practices that were initially designed to favor certain groups or to exclude others. In such situations, inertia is a powerful barrier to change.

Anti-discrimination laws have reduced but not eliminated discrimination. The research reviewed in Chapter 2 indicates that employers continue to discriminate in hiring, job assignment, and promotions. Over the past decade, anti-discrimination laws appear to have become less effective remedies. Since 1985, only one in seven discrimination complaints to the EEOC charged hiring discrimination; most charged discrimination in terminations (Donohue and Siegelman 1991, figure 6).[48] As noted, job applicants who are not hired seldom have enough information to know whether discrimination occurred, hence most victims of hiring discrimination probably do not complain.[49] Meanwhile, the growing number of people complaining of discrimination in terminations may be a disincentive to employers to hire minorities and women. If anti-discrimination laws have become less effective in deterring hiring discrimination and employees are reluctant to sue their current employers over promotion discrimination, affirmative action is the primary mechanism to reduce hiring and promotion discrimination (Donohue and Siegelman 1991, p. 1033).

87

Discrimination is an expensive business practice. For example, after taking into account characteristics that affect workers' productivity, job segregation is estimated to reduce minority men's annual earnings, on average, by at least $1,500 and women's earnings by at least $3,400 (Bergmann 1996, p. 40). According to the most comprehensive study available, sex segregation accounts for 89 percent of the earnings gap between the sexes (Petersen and Morgan 1995). And because discrimination keeps workers from being assigned to jobs based on their ability, it is also costly to employers and stockholders.

Affirmative action is a potentially strong weapon in the arsenal of anti-discrimination weapons. Outlawing discrimination has not been sufficient to eliminate it. Discriminatory employment practices raise the unemployment and underemployment rates of minority men and women, and reduce the chances of job advancement for all women and minority men relative to white men. As long as employment practices perpetuate race and gender discrimination in the workplace, affirmative action policies and programs will be needed.

IS AFFIRMATIVE ACTION EFFECTIVE IN REDUCING SEX AND RACE DISCRIMINATION?

Are the practices that constitute affirmative action powerful enough to eradicate both intentional and structural discrimination without imposing undue costs on business in lost productivity? This is a tall order for a social policy. And it is an especially tall order for the Federal contract compliance program, the only mandated affirmative action program for private firms. The Federal contract compliance program applies to a minority of employers; it does not require any specific outcomes as long as employers reportedly make a good faith effort; its enforcement depends entirely on a President's stance on affirmative action so it has been haphazardly enforced; and its primary sanction—debarment from

Federal contracts—has rarely been imposed. In short, the presidential executive order requiring affirmative action of Federal contractors is a weak policy. Nonetheless, the available evidence indicates that affirmative action has been effective. The combination of affirmative action required by Federal and state governments, court-ordered affirmative action, voluntary efforts, and the Federal contract compliance program have reduced race and sex discrimination.

Even with full commitment of enforcement agencies and employers, affirmative action alone cannot eradicate all race and sex discrimination in employment. It will be most effective in preventing discrimination' and creating a fair and open labor market when the economy is healthy and when other programs are implemented to enhance the skills that minorities and women bring to and acquire in the labor force. The latter programs must ensure that our nation's schools and workplaces give youths the chance to acquire skills that will enable them to participate fully in the nation's economy, regardless of their race, ethnicity, sex, and economic class.

WHAT PRACTICES ARE MOST EFFECTIVE?

As indicated above, the contract compliance program has been most effective when it has had the support of the President of the United States, when the Office for Federal Contract Compliance Programs has had sufficient resources, and when the economy has been growing. When policymakers, regulators, and employers have been serious about affirmative action, it has curtailed discrimination against traditionally excluded groups. The across-the-board effects of the contract compliance program, while modest, have been commensurate with the scope of the executive order's mandate and the OFCCP's resources. Affirmative action works best when it is mandated and it includes goals, monitoring, and the possibility of serious sanctions.

89

HOW DOES AFFIRMATIVE ACTION AFFECT WHITES, MEN, COMMERCE, AND AMERICAN SOCIETY?

Affirmative action does not replace one form of favoritism with another; it replaces cronyism with objective personnel practices. Its successes have not been achieved through discrimination against white men. Federally mandated affirmative action programs neither require nor allow employers to give preference to workers because of their sex or race. Giving preference to an unqualified or less qualified candidate because of her or his race or sex constitutes illegal discrimination, regardless of whether the beneficiary is male or female, white or minority. In the early 1970s, some employers reserved a specific number of jobs for women and minorities, but this practice virtually disappeared after the courts ruled that it violated the 1964 anti-discrimination law. While the affirmative action efforts of some contemporary employers are undoubtedly unfair to individual whites or men, reverse discrimination is rare.

Eliminating informal, personalistic hiring and job assignment practices benefits white men who lack the advantage of family, school, or social ties. Because affirmative action practices enhance all employees' access to fair procedures and due process, it is a force for fairness and meritocracy. It is not surprising, then, that more employers, managers, and workers in affirmative action firms support such practices than oppose them.

Available research evidence indicates that affirmative action does not reduce firms' productivity or profitability. To the contrary, personnel practices associated with affirmative action improve firms' efficiency by ensuring that workers are assigned to jobs based on their ability. Although there are costs associated with affirmative action, it is cheaper than discrimination.

One recurrent question is whether affirmative action is a divisive policy that exacerbates conflict between the races and sexes. While

90

public discourse has sometimes been vitriolic, it has misconstrued the realities of affirmative action. Although polls indicate that few Americans feel very strongly about affirmative action, most Americans support race-targeted intervention programs designed to allow minorities to compete fairly. For example, for at least two decades about 70 percent of whites have endorsed affirmative action when pollsters ask about what it actually involves: genuine efforts to broaden the applicant pools to include more qualified women and minorities.

Although the majority of Americans approve of most of the employment practices that affirmative action entails, many do not realize this because they misunderstand what affirmative action employers do. Many Americans think that affirmative action is a "numbers game" in which employers select minorities or women solely to meet goals. Adding to the confusion is the fact that employers sometimes cite affirmative action as a face-saving explanation for rejecting less qualified white or male candidates. The effect of this practice extends to everyone who hears about it second or third hand. Of survey respondents who believe that a white person will lose out on a job or promotion to an equally or less qualified African American, few held this opinion based on personal experience; most heard about it through someone else or through the media (Steeh and Krysan 1996, pp. 139–40). In addition, sex and race stereotypes persuade many Americans that women or minorities are excluded from jobs because they are unqualified or disinterested, and not because of discrimination. These factors, in combination with political opponents and media accounts misrepresenting or misunderstanding what affirmative action is or exaggerating whites' opposition to it are largely responsible for affirmative action's image as divisive and controversial.

91

CONCLUSION

Despite the impact of anti-discrimination laws on job integration and the good-faith efforts of many employers to diversify their workforces, the strength of habit in people's ways of thinking and organizations' ways of doing business means that more concerted efforts are necessary to eliminate discriminatory barriers. Weakening or ending affirmative action at the very least would slow the progress that minorities and women have made in entering the economic mainstream. The erosion in the relative economic standing of African Americans during the 1980s stemmed in part from the hiatus in affirmative action enforcement. Without government pressure for affirmative action, cronyism will reign supreme, and those protected by affirmative action as well as others who lack the right connections will stand to lose. Eliminating affirmative action will increase job discrimination based on sex and race and the wage gap between white men and other groups.

The major problem associated with affirmative action revealed in the research reviewed here is a problem of too little, not too much. Many employment practices still discriminate against men of color and all women, and anti-discrimination law provides a possible remedy only after the damage has been done. The fact that the law also makes the victims of discrimination responsible for enforcement reduces society's ability to eradicate discrimination because victims lack the information and economic resources necessary for legal action. After-the-fact interventions are expensive for employers as well as workers, as evidenced by the huge costs associated with losing or settling class-action lawsuits. In contrast, affirmative action can prevent discrimination by encouraging employers to pursue objective and open personnel practices.

The effects of affirmative action on its intended beneficiaries are commensurate with the scope of the Federal affirmative action program and employers' voluntary efforts. The more resources allocated for enforcement and the more monitoring, the more effective affirmative action is in preventing discrimination. As long as the enforcement of the only Federally-mandated affirmative action regulations depends on who occupies the White House, requiring affirmative action of Federal contractors will remain an unreliable way to prevent discrimination, even among Federal contractors. Statutory approaches to eliminating discrimination are potentially stronger because their mandate is not subject to politics, and their scope can be far broader.

We encourage the media to educate the public and employers to educate their workers about the true nature of affirmative action. Most public opposition to affirmative action is based on misconceptions, and the media share responsibility for these misconceptions. Opposition to affirmative action is likely to be influenced by three myths. The first is that race and sex discrimination no longer exists. The second is that affirmative action involves quotas and preferences that reduce the opportunities available to groups not targeted for affirmative action. The third is that affirmative action undermines meritocratic employment practices. Fuller media coverage of ongoing discrimination, of what affirmative action actually entails, and of its negligible negative effects on majority-group members and U.S. business will improve its prospects for success.[49]

Although many Americans would prefer a labor market that never takes race or gender into account, as long as employers and employment practices routinely discriminate against minorities and women, the choice is not between meritocracy and affirmative action, it is between discrimination and affirmative action.

ENDNOTES

[1] For positions that are filled from within an establishment, the labor pool includes workers in the jobs from which workers are promoted.

[2] This includes about 100,000 construction firms and 93,000 nonconstruction firms (U.S. Department of Labor, Office of Federal Contract Compliance 1996, p. 1).

[3] Executive Order 11375 added "sex" and changed "creed" to "religion."

[4] According to Section 706(g), a court that finds an employer, labor union, or employment agency guilty of unlawful discrimination "may enjoin the [defendant] from engaging in such unlawful practice, and order such affirmative action as may be appropriate" (Burstein 1995, p.11).

[5] The following safeguards must be in place before quotas can be used. First, a quota may apply only to specified jobs. Second, the quota must be temporary, operating only until the court's ruling is satisfied. Third, the employer must be allowed to hire members of the majority group if it cannot find qualified members of the targeted group. Fourth, the quota must not rule out majority-group members' chances for jobs or promotions. Fifth, the quota must be the only way to end the illegal discrimination. This fifth condition is met in cases in which employers or unions have persisted in discriminating in defiance of a court order.

[6] In the early 1980s, for instance, courts ordered quotas in just 51 cases.

[7] Firms' affirmative action policies and practices apply only to their regular employees, not to temporary workers, leased workers, independent contractors, contracted workers— categories that may employ growing numbers of workers (Kalleberg et al. 1997).

[8] Another 41 percent said that their employers did not engage in affirmative action, and 15 percent of respondents did not know if their employers practiced affirmative action. Of the workers who answered the question, 51 percent said that their employer practiced affirmative hiring and promotion (Taylor 1995, p.1389).

[9] New York state made race discrimination illegal in 1945; by 1961 half of the U.S. population lived in states with enforceable laws prohibiting race discrimination in employment (Graham 1992, p. 52; Burstein 1998, pp. 63–4).

[10] Occupational race and sex segregation do not stem solely from discrimination; they are also affected by sex and race differences in education, training, and workers' preferences (Reskin 1993). However, researchers agree that employers' practices contribute to the levels of race and sex segregation. As we will see below, the jobs in which minorities and women are concentrated pay less and offer fewer promotion opportunities than do the jobs that white men dominate (England and McCreary 1987; Jacobs and Steinberg 1990; Glass and Camarigg 1992), and hence are unlikely to be more attractive to workers of color and white women than white men.

[11] The data do not permit comparing the sexes within racial groups.

[12] Of particular importance is Title VII of the 1964 Civil Rights Act, which banned discrimination on the basis of race, color, religion, sex, or national origin in hiring, job assignments, promotions, layoffs, and pay.

[13] For other examples of discrimination cases from the 1990s, see U.S. Department of Labor, Employment Standards Administration, Office of Federal Contract Compliance Programs (1996).

[14] For a discussion of the methodological issues associated with measuring discrimination through employment audits, see Heckman and Siegelman (1993).

[15] Also, workers probably hesitate to recommend people of the "wrong" race and sex.

[16] More than 40 percent of Chicago employers interviewed by William Julius Wilson's (1996, p. 133–4) research team never advertised entry-level jobs in the newspaper; others did so only when employees' referrals did not turn up enough applicants.

[17] Evaluation bias means that women and minorities have to outperform white men to be evaluated as their equals (Foschi 1992, p. 198; Fiske et al. 1991). A study of managers and professionals employed by a Fortune 500 company illustrates this point: Although all of the managers had been rated above average in performance, supervisors rated the African Americans lower on their promotion potential than whites with the same education, seniority, organizational level, and job type (Landau 1995).

[18] Unless organizations that change their policies also change their formal structures, inertia can prevent the managers from changing their behaviors (Baron 1991, p. 133).

[19] These nonstandard work arrangements include part-time work, temporary work, on-call work, and contract work (Kalleberg et al. 1997).

[20] The U.S. Civil Rights Commission, the General Accounting Office, committees of both Houses of Congress, and the courts have all concurred that the OFCCP has failed to make effective use of the sanctions at its disposal (Leonard 1994, p. 30).

[21] One indication of the changing enforcement climate was that OFCCP administrators discouraged staff members from pressing federal contractors to set goals and timetables; and as a result, their use declined (Blumrosen 1993, p. 274).

[22] In 1994, 68 agencies had filed affirmative employment plans with the EEOC (Stephanopoulos and Edley 1995).

[23] For a definition of the segregation index, see Chapter 2.

[24] Between 1970 and 1990 the index of race segregation declined from 38.3 to 28.6 among men and from 36.6 to 25.3 among women. During the same period, the index of sex segregation fell from 67.9 to 51.9 among African Americans and from 67.6 to 60.2 among whites (Reskin, Hickey, and Wheeler 1998).

[25] African-American and white women have made little headway in the skilled trades. Only 0.8 percent of African-American women and one percent of white women held craft occupations in 1970; twenty years later, their representation had inched up to 2.3 and 2.1 percent (U.S. Bureau of the Census 1972, 1992).

[26] In 1980, the U.S. Census Bureau renamed clerical occupations "administrative support" occupations. The administrative-support category largely comprises clerical occupations.

[27] During the same period, the percentage of black men employed in clerical occupations rose from 5 to 9 percent (U.S. Bureau of the Census 1963, Table 3).

[28] Smith and Welch (1984) speculated, based on data for federal contractors, that employers reclassified some customarily female jobs as managerial to give the impression of more advancement for female employees.

[29] These rates are consistent with the modest effects of affirmative action reported above.

[30] Male research subjects who were told that they were chosen for a leadership role solely on the basis of their sex disregarded this information. Their failure to express any ill effects at having been selected entirely because of their sex may stem from the fact that they rejected this as implausible (Heilman et al. 1987; Major et al. 1994, p. 138). Other experimental research suggests that believing that one's selection was based entirely on preference has negative psychological consequences for experimental subjects with low self-esteem (Heilman et al. 1990).

[31] Unfortunately, experimental studies have not compared the psychological effects of selection-based merit plus sex or race with the effects of sex- or race-based rejection, which remains the most likely alternative.

[32] The greater progress in integrating male-dominated jobs in California state agencies headed by women than those run by men may reflect female leaders' generally higher commitment to sex integration (Baron 1991, p. 130).

[33] How both targeted and nontargeted groups respond to affirmative action depends partly on whether they perceive it to be fair (Nacoste 1990; Kravitz et al. 1997).

[34] Although line managers preferred identity-neutral affirmative action procedures (i.e., those that do not target specific groups), they did not oppose procedures that take race or sex into account, and procedures that take race or sex into account did not adversely affect managers' attitudes toward their employer (Konrad and Linnehan 1995b, pp. 424, 448).

[35] Through 1993, only 35 contractors had been debarred (Leonard 1994, pp. 29–30).

[36] Edelman and Petterson's (1993, p. 29) survey of 207 firms found that whether a firm's efforts were voluntary or the result of external pressure was unrelated to changes in women's or minorities' representation in its workforce, perhaps because this factor did not affect whether firms implemented affirmative action recruitment or training programs.

[37] Lynch's (1989, p. 53) search for white male Southern Californians who saw themselves as victims of reverse discrimination turned up only 32 men.

[38] Younger whites, those from more privileged backgrounds, and those from areas with larger black populations—especially black populations who were relatively well off—were the most likely to believe that blacks benefited from preferential treatment (Taylor 1994b)

[39] Two percent were by white men charging sex, race, or national-origin discrimination (three-quarters of these charged sex discrimination), and 1.8 percent were by white women

charging race discrimination (Blumrosen 1996, p. 5).

[40] In the early years of affirmative action, some federal contractors implemented quotas; since then the OFCCP has made considerable effort to ensure that contractors understand that quotas are illegal.

[41] Occupational segregation by sex, race, and ethnicity no doubt contribute to this perception by reinforcing the notion that one's sex, color, or ethnicity is naturally related to the ability to perform a particular job.

[42] The disproportionate number of court-ordered interventions to curtail race and sex discrimination in cities' police and fire departments (Martin 1991) and the large number of court challenges by white men (Bureau of National Affairs 1995, pp. 5–12) probably contributed to the public's impression that hiring quotas are common.

[43] No data were provided on the proportion who believed that affirmative action hampered productivity.

[44] Although firms' stock prices fall after the media report a discrimination suit, they rebound within a few days (Hersch 1991; Wright et al. 1995).

[45] The $26 billion estimate includes the budgets of the OFCCP, the EEOC, other Federal agencies' affirmative action related activities, and private firms' compliance costs estimated at $20 million for each million of public funds budgeted for enforcement (Brimelow and Spencer 1993). Arguably, the EEOC's budget—indeed all enforcement costs—should be chalked up to the cost of discrimination, not the cost of affirmative action.

[46] Several factors affect Americans' response to surveys about affirmative action in the workplace: whether their employer practices affirmative action (Taylor 1995), their own conception of what affirmative action means (one-third of white respondents to a 1995 CBS/New York Times poll acknowledged that they were not sure what affirmative action is; Steeh and Krysan 1996, p. 129), whether the question also asks about affirmative action in education, whether the question asks about race- or sex-based affirmative action (although contractors are also obliged to provide affirmative action for Vietnam-era veterans and disabled persons, these groups are invisible in opinion polls), the respondents' own race and sex, the reasons respondents think racial inequality exists, and their level of racial prejudice (Bobo and Kluegel 1993). For full reviews, see Steeh and Krysan (1996) and Kravitz et al. (1997).

[47] Only one percent of respondents named affirmative action as the most important problem our country faces (Entman 1997, p. 38).

[48] Promotion cases are rare, given employees' reluctance to charge their current employers (Donohue and Siegelman 1991, p. 1031).

[49] There is no evidence regarding whether this differs for victims between conventional and "reverse" discrimination.

REFERENCES

American Psychological Association. 1987. "In the Supreme Court of the United States: Clara Watson v. Fort Worth Bank and Trust, *Amicus Curiae* Brief." [Reprinted in 1988 *The American Psychologist* 43:1019–1028.]

Ashenfelter, Orley and James Heckman. 1976. "Measuring the Effect of an Anti-Discrimination Program." Pp. 46–84 in *Evaluating the Labor Market Effects of Social Programs,* edited by O. Ashenfelter and J. Blum. Princeton, NJ: Princeton University Press.

Badgett, M. V. Lee and Heidi Hartmann. 1995. "The Effectiveness of Equal Employment Opportunity Policies." Pp. 55–97 in *Economic Perspectives on Affirmative Action,* edited by M. C. Simms. Washington, DC: Joint Center for Political and Economic Studies.

Baldi, Stephane and Debra B. McBrier. 1997. "Do the Determinants of Promotion Differ for Blacks and Whites?" *Work and Occupations* 24:478–97.

Baron, James N. 1991. "Organizational Evidence of Ascription in Labor Markets." Pp. 113–43 in *New Approaches to Economic and Social Analyses of Discrimination*, edited by R. R. Cornwall and P. V. Wunnava. New York: Praeger.

Baron, James N. and William T. Bielby. 1985. "Organizational Barriers to Gender Equality: Sex Segregation of Jobs and Opportunities." Pp. 233–51 in *Gender and the Life Course*, edited by A. S. Rossi. New York: Aldine.

Baron, James N., Alison Davis-Blake, and William T. Bielby. 1986. "The Structure of Opportunity: How Promotion Ladders Vary within and among Organizations." *Administrative Science Quarterly* 31:248–73.

Baron, James N., Brian S. Mittman, and Andrew E. Newman. 1991. "Targets of Opportunity: Organizational and Environmental Determinants of Gender Integration within the California Civil Service, 1979–1985." *American Journal of Sociology* 96:1362–1401.

Becker, Gary S. 1971. *A Theory of Discrimination.* 2d ed. Chicago, IL: University of Chicago Press.

Bell, Ella and Stella M. Nkomo. 1994. Barriers to Work Place Advancement Experienced by African Americans. Paper prepared for the Glass Ceiling Commission, U.S. Department of Labor, Washington, DC.

Beller, Andrea. 1982. "Occupational Segregation by Sex: Determinants and Changes." *Journal of Human Resources* 17:371–92.

Bendick, Marc, Jr. 1992. "Discrimination against Latino Job Applicants: A Controlled Experiment." Washington, DC: Fair Employment Council of Greater Washington.

———. 1997. *Declaration.* Statement Submitted to the Supreme Court of California in Response to Proposition 209, September 26.

Bendick, Marc, Jr. and Mary Lou Egan. 1988. *Jobs: Employment Opportunities in the Washington Area for Persons with Limited Employment Qualifications.* Washington, DC: Greater Washington Research Center.

Bergmann, Barbara R. 1996. *In Defense of Affirmative Action.* New York: Basic Books.

Bielby, William T. and James N. Baron. 1984. "A Woman's Place Is with Other Women: Sex Segregation within Organizations." Pp. 27–55 in *Sex Segregation in the Workplace,* edited by B. F. Reskin. Washington, DC: National Academy Press.

———. 1986. "Men and Women at Work: Sex Segregation and Statistical Discrimination." *American Journal of Sociology* 91:759–99.

Bills, David B. 1988. "Educational Credentials and Hiring Decisions: What Employers Look for in New Employees." *Research in Social Stratification and Mobility* 7:71–97.

Black Firefighters Assn. of Dallas v. City of Dallas, 19 F.3d 992 (1994).

Blair-Loy, Mary. 1996. "Career Patterns of Executive Women in Finance: An Optimal Matching Analysis." Department of Sociology, University of Chicago, Chicago, IL. Unpublished manuscript.

Blumrosen, Alfred W. 1993. *Modern Law.* Madison, WI: University of Wisconsin Press.

———. 1996. *Declaration.* Statement Submitted to the Supreme Court of California in Response to Proposition 209, September 26.

Bobo, Lawrence D. 1996. *Declaration.* Statement Submitted to the Supreme Court of California in Response to Proposition 209, November 1.

———. 1997. "The Color Line, the Dilemma, and the Dream." Pp. 31–55 in *Civil Rights and Social Wrongs: Black-White Relations since World War II,* edited by J. Higham. University Park, PA: Pennsylvania State University Press.

Bobo, Lawrence and Vincent L. Hutchings. 1996. "Perceptions of Racial Group Competition: Extending Blumer's Theory of Group Position to a Multiracial Social Context." *American Sociological Review* 61:951–72.

Bobo, Lawrence and James R. Kluegel. 1993. "Opposition to Race Targeting." *American Sociological Review* 58:443–64.

Bobo, Larry and Susan A. Suh. 1996. "Surveying Racial Discrimination: Analyses from a Multi-Ethnic Labor Market." Working Paper No. 75, Russell Sage Foundation, New York.

Bobo, Lawrence D., Camille L. Zubrinsky, James H. Johnson, and Melvin L. Oliver. 1994. "Public Opinion before and after a Spring of Discontent." Pp. 103–33 in *The Los Angeles Riots*, edited by M. Baldassare. Boulder, CO: Westview.

Braddock, Jomills Henry and James M. McPartland. 1987. "How Minorities Continue to Be Excluded from Equal Employment Opportunities: Research on Labor Market and Institutional Barriers." *Journal of Social Issues* 43:5–39.

Brass, Daniel. 1985. "Men's and Women's Networks: A Study of Interaction Patterns and Influence in Organizations." *Academy of Management Journal* 28:327–43.

Brimelow, Peter and Leslie Spencer. 1993. "When Quotas Replace Merit, Everybody Suffers." *Forbes,* February 15, pp. 80–102.

Brimmer, Andrew F. 1995. "The Economic Cost of Discrimination against Black Americans." Pp. 11–29 in *Economic Perspectives on Affirmative Action*, edited by M. C. Simms. Washington, DC: Joint Center for Political and Economic Studies.

Browne, Irene. 1998. "Introduction." In *Race, Gender, and Economic Inequality: Latina and African American Women in the U.S. Labor Market*. New York: Russell Sage.

Browne, Irene and Cynthia Hewitt. 1995. "Networks, Discrimination, and Location: Explaining Job Segregation among African Americans." Paper presented at the Multi-City SUI Conference, New York.

Bruno, Andorra. 1995. *Affirmative Action in Employment*. CRS Report for Congress. Washington, DC: Congressional Research Service.

Bureau of National Affairs. 1986a. *Affirmative Action Today: A Legal and Practical Analysis. A BNA Special Report*. Washington, DC: The Bureau of National Affairs.

———. 1986b. *EEO Policies and Programs*. Personnel Policies Forum Survey No. 141. Washington, DC: The Bureau of National Affairs.

———. 1995. *Affirmative Action after Adarand: A Legal, Regulatory, Legislative Outlook*. Washington, DC: The Bureau of National Affairs.

Burstein, Paul. 1985. *Discrimination, Jobs, and Politics*. Chicago, IL: University of Chicago Press.

———. 1991. "'Reverse Discrimination' Cases in the Federal Courts: Mobilization by a Countermovement." *Sociological Quarterly* 32:511–28.

———. 1995. "The Impact of EEO Law: A Social Movement Perspective." Paper presented at a Conference on the Civil Rights Act of 1964, Washington, DC.

———. 1998. *Discrimination, Jobs, and Politics*. Rev. ed. Chicago, IL: University of Chicago Press.

Butler, John Sibley. 1996. "Myrdal Revisited: The Negro in Business, the Professions, Public Service, and Other White Collar Occupations." Pp. 138–68 in *An American Dilemma Revisited*, edited by O. Clayton, Jr. New York: Russell Sage Foundation.

Carnoy, Martin. 1994. *Faded Dreams: The Politics and Economics of Race in America*. New York: Cambridge University Press.

Carnoy, Martin and Richard Rothstein. 1996. *Hard Lessons*. Washington, DC: Economic Policy Institute.

Carrington, William J. and Kenneth R. Troske. 1994. "Gender Segregation in Small Firms." *Journal of Human Resources* 30:503–33.

———. 1998a. "Sex Segregation across U.S. Manufacturing." *Industrial and Labor Relations Review* 51:445–64.

———. 1998b. "Interfirm Segregation and the Black/White Wage Gap." *Journal of Labor Economics* 16:231–60.

Cassirer, Naomi R. and Barbara F. Reskin. 1998. "The Effect of Organizational Context on Women's and Men's Attachment to Their Jobs." Department of Sociology, Notre Dame University, South Bend, IN. Unpublished manuscript.

Catalyst. 1996. *Women in Corporate Leadership*. New York: Catalyst.

Citizens' Commission on Civil Rights. 1984. *Affirmative Action to Open the Doors of Job Opportunity*. Washington, DC: Commission on Civil Rights.

Cohen, Lisa E., Joseph P. Broschak, and Heather A. Haveman. Forthcoming. "And Then There Were More? The Effect of Organizational Sex Composition on Hiring and Promotion." *American Sociological Review*.

Collins, Sharon M. 1989. "The Marginalization of Black Executives." *Social Problems* 36:317–31.

———. 1993. "Blacks on the Bubble: The Vulnerability of Black Executives in White Corporations." *Sociological Quarterly* 34:429–47.

———. 1997. *Black Corporate Executives. The Making and Breaking of the Black Middle Class*. Philadelphia, PA: Temple.

Conrad, Cecilia. 1995. "The Economic Cost of Affirmative Action." Pp. 33–53 in *Economic Perspectives on Affirmative Action*, edited by M. C. Simms. Washington, DC: Joint Center for Political and Economic Studies.

Cox, Taylor H. and Stacy Blake. 1991. "Managing Cultural Diversity: Implications for Organizational Competitiveness." *Academy of Management Executive* 5:45–56.

Cox, Taylor H. and Stella M. Nkomo. 1986. "Differential Performance Appraisal Criteria: A Field Study of Black and White Managers." *Group & Organization Studies* 11:101–19.

———. 1991. "A Race and Gender-Group Analysis of Early Career Experience of MBAs." *Work and Occupations* 18:431–46.

Crocker, Jennifer and Brenda Major. 1989. "Social Stigma and Self-Esteem: The Self-Protective Properties of Stigma." *Psychological Review* 96:608–30.

Crosby, Faye J. and Sharon D. Herzberger. 1996. "For Affirmative Action." Pp. 3–109 in *Affirmative Action: Pros and Cons of Policy and Practice*, edited by R. J. Simon. Washington, DC: American University Press.

Cross, Harry, with Genevieve Kenney, Jane Mell, and Wendy Zimmerman. 1990. "Employer Hiring Practices: Differential Treatment of Hispanic and Anglo Job Seekers." Urban Institute Report 90-4, The Urban Institute, Washington, DC.

Darley, John M. and Russel H. Fazio. 1980. "Expectancy Confirmation Sequences." *American Psychologist* 35:367–81.

Davis, James A. and Tom W. Smith. 1994. *General Social Survey* [MRDF]. Chicago, IL: National Opinion Research Center [producer, distributor].

———. 1996. *General Social Survey* [MRDF]. Chicago, IL: National Opinion Research Center [producer, distributor].

Deaux, Kay and Joseph C. Ullman. 1983. *Women of Steel*. New York: Praeger.

DiPrete, Thomas. 1987. "The Professionalization of Administration and Equal Opportunity in the U.S. Federal Government." *American Journal of Sociology* 93:119–40.

———. 1989. *The Bureaucratic Labor Market*. New York: Plenum.

DiTomaso, Nancy. 1993. "Notes on Xerox Case: Balanced Work Force at Xerox." School of Management, Rutgers University, New Brunswick, NJ. Unpublished manuscript.

Dobbin, Frank, Lauren Edelman, John W. Meyer, W. Richard Scott, and Ann Swidler. 1988. "The Expansion of Due Process in Organizations." Pp. 71–100 in *Institutional Patterns and Organizations: Culture and Environment*, edited by L. G. Zucker. Cambridge, MA: Ballinger.

Dobbin, Frank, John Sutton, John Meyer, and W. Richard Scott. 1993. "Equal Opportunity Law and the Construction of Internal Labor Markets." *American Journal of Sociology* 99:396–427.

Dobrzynski, Judith H. 1996. "Study Finds Few Women in 5 Highest Company Jobs." *The New York Times*. October 18, p. C3.

Donohue, John J. 1986. "Is Title VII Efficient?" *University of Pennsylvania Law Review* 134:1411–31.

Donohue John J. and James Heckman. 1991. "Re-evaluating Federal Civil Rights Policy." *Georgetown Law Review* 79:1713–35.

Donohue, John J. and Peter Siegelman. 1991. "The Changing Nature of Employment Discrimination Litigation." *Stanford Law Review* 43:983–1033.

Duke, Lynne. 1993. "Shoney's Bias Settlement Sends $105 Million Signal." *Washington Post* , February 5, pp. A1, A20.

Durr, Marlese and John R. Logan. 1997. "Racial Submarkets in Government Employment: African American Managers in New York State." *Sociological Forum* 12:353–70.

Eberhardt, Jennifer L. and Susan T. Fiske. 1996. "Motivating Individuals to Change: What Is a Target to Do?" Pp. 369–415 in *Stereotypes and Sterotyping*, edited by C. N. MacRae, C. Stangor, and M. Hewstone. New York: Guilford Press.

Edelman, Lauren B. 1992. "Legal Ambiguity and Symbolic Structures: Organizational Mediation of Civil Rights Law." *American Journal of Sociology* 97:1531–76.

Edelman, Lauren B., Steven E. Abraham, and Howard S. Erlanger. 1992. "Professional Construction of the Legal Environment: The Inflated Threat of Wrongful Discharge Doctrine." *Law and Society Review* 26:47–83.

Edelman, Lauren B. and Stephen Petterson. 1993. "Symbols and Substance in Organizational Response to Civil Rights Law." Paper presented at the annual meeting of the American Sociological Association, August 13–17, Miami Beach, FL.

Edelman, Lauren B., Stephen Petterson, Elizabeth Chambliss, and Howard S. Erlanger. 1991. "Legal Ambiguity and the Politics of Compliance: Affirmative Action Officers' Dilemma." *Law and Policy* 13:73–97.

England, Paula and Lori McCreary. 1987. "Gender Inequality in Paid Employment." Pp. 286–320 in *Analyzing Gender*, edited by B. Hess and M. M. Ferree. Beverly Hills, CA: Russell Sage.

Entman, Robert M. 1997. "Manufacturing Discord: Media in the Affirmative Action Debate." *Press/Politics* 2:32–51.

Erdreich, Ben, Beth Slavet, and Antonio Amador. 1996. *Fair and Equitable Treatment: A Progress Report on Minority Employment in the Federal Government*. Washington, DC: U.S. Merit Systems Protection Board.

Fair Employment Council of Greater Washington. 1992. "Measuring Employment Discrimination through Controlled Experiments." Washington, DC:
Fair Employment Council of Greater Washington.

Fisher, Ann B. 1985. "Businessmen Like to Hire by the Numbers." *Fortune
Magazine*, September 16, pp. 26, 28–30.

Fiske, Susan T. and S. E. Taylor. 1991. "Social Inference." Chap. 9 in *Social
Cognition*. New York: McGraw-Hill.

Fiske, Susan T., Donald N. Bersoff, Eugene Borgida, Kay Deaux, and Madeline
E. Heilman. 1991. "Social Science Research on Trial: Use of Sex Stereotyping Research in Price Waterhouse v. Hopkins." *American Psychologist*
46:1049–60.

Fix, Michael and Raymond J. Struyk, eds. 1993. *Clear and Convincing
Evidence. Measurement of Discrimination in America*. Washington, DC:
The Urban Institute.

Ford, J. Kevin, Kurt Kraiger, and Susan L. Schectman. 1986. "Study of Race
Effects in Objective Indices and Subjective Evaluations of Performance: A
Meta-Analysis of Performance Criteria." *Psychological Bulletin* 99:330–37.

Foschi, Martha. 1992. "Gender and Double Standards for Competence." Pp.
181–207 in *Gender Interaction and Inequality*, edited by C. L. Ridgeway.
New York: Springer-Verlag.

Foschi, Martha, Larissa Lai, and Kirsten Sigerson. 1994. "Gender and Double
Standards in the Assessment of Male and Female Job Applicants." *Social
Psychology Quarterly* 57:326–39.

Friedman, Raymond A. and Caitlin Deinard. 1996. "Black Caucus Groups at
Xerox Corporation." Pp. 300–13 in *Managerial Excellence through Diversity: Text and Cases*, edited by M. Gentile. Chicago, IL: Irwin.

Gamson, William A. and Andre Modigliani. 1987. "The Changing Culture of
Affirmative Action." *Research in Political Sociology* 3:137–77.

Gerber, Gwendolyn L. 1989. "The More Positive Evaluation of Men than
Women on Gender-Stereotyped Traits." *Psychological Reports* 65:275–86.

Gill, Andrew W. 1989. "The Role of Discrimination in Determining Occupational Structure." *Industrial and Labor Relations Review* 42:610–23.

Glass Ceiling Commission. See U.S. Department of Labor, Office of Federal
Contract Compliance Programs, Glass Ceiling Commission.

Glass, Jennifer and Valerie Camarigg. 1992. "Gender, Parenthood, and Job-
Family Compatibility." *American Journal of Sociology* 98:131–51.

Graham, Hugh Davis. 1990. *The Civil Rights Era*. New York: Oxford University Press.

————. 1992. "The Origins of Affirmative Action: Civil Rights and the Regulatory State." *Annals of the American Academy of Political and Social Science* 523:50–62.

Greenhaus, Jeffrey H., Saroj Parasuraman, and Wayne M. Wormley. 1990. "Effects of Race on Organizational Experiences, Job Performance Evaluations, and Career Outcomes." *Academy of Management Journal* 33:64–86.

Gross, Edward. 1968. *"Plus ça change...?* The Sexual Structure of Occupations over Time." *Social Problems* 16:198–208.

Hall, Francine S. and Maryann H. Albrecht. 1979. *The Management of Affirmative Action.* Santa Monica, CA: Goodyear Publishing.

Harrison, Roderick J. and Claudette E. Bennett. 1995. "Racial and Ethnic Diversity." Pp. 141–210 in *State of the Union: America in the 1990s*, vol. 2, *Social Trends*, edited by R. Farley. New York: Russell Sage.

Hartmann, Heidi. 1996. "How Much Have Women Benefited from Affirmative Action in Employment?" Pp. 77–96 in *The Affirmative Action Debate*, edited by G. Curry. Reading, MA: Addison-Wesley.

Harvard Law Review. 1989. "Rethinking Weber: The Business Response to Affirmative Action." *Harvard Law Review* 102:658–71.

Heckman, James and Brook Payner. 1989. "Determining the Impact of Federal Antidiscrimination Policy on the Economic Status of Blacks." *American Economic Review* 65:158–68.

Heckman, James J. and Peter Siegelman. 1993. "The Urban Institute Audit Studies: Their Methods and Findings." Pp. 187–229 in *Clear and Convincing Evidence: Measurement of Discrimination in America*, edited by M. Fix and R. J. Struyk. Washington, DC: The Urban Institute.

Heckman, James J. and Kenneth Wolpin. 1976. "Does the Contract Compliance Program Work? An Analysis of Chicago Data." *Industrial and Labor Relations Review* 29:544–64.

Heilman, Madeline E. 1984. "Information as a Deterrent against Sex Discrimination: The Effects of Applicant Sex and Information Type on Employment Decisions." *Organizational Behavior and Human Performance* 33:175–86.

————. 1994. "Affirmative Action: Some Unintended Consequences for Working Women." *Research in Organizational Behavior* 16:125–69.

————. 1995. "Sex Stereotypes and Their Effects in the Workplace: What We Know and What We Don't Know." *Journal of Social Behavior and Personality* 10:3–26.

Heilman, Madeline E., Caryn J. Block, and Jonathan A. Lucas. 1992. "Presumed Incompetent? Stigmatization and Affirmative Action Efforts." *Journal of Applied Psychology* 77:536–44.

Heilman, Madeline E., Jonathan A. Lucas, and Stella Kaplow. 1990. "Self-Derogating Consequences of Sex-Based Preferential Selection: The Moderating Role of Initial Self-Confidence." *Organizational Behavior and Human Decision Processes* 46:202–16.

Heilman, Madeline E., Michael C. Simon, and David R. Repper. 1987. "Intentionally Favored, Unintentionally Harmed? Impact of Sex-Based Preferential Selection on Self-Perceptions and Self-Evaluations." *Journal of Applied Psychology* 72:62–8.

Hellerstein, Judith K., David Neumark, and Kenneth R. Troske. 1998. "Market Forces and Sex Discrimination." Department of Sociology, University of Maryland, College Park. Unpublished manuscript.

Hersch, Joni. 1991. "Equal Employment Opportunity Law and Firm Profitability." *Journal of Human Resources* 26:139–53.

Hill, Herbert and James E. Jones, Jr. 1993. *Race in America.* Madison, WI: University of Wisconsin.

Hitt, Michael A. and Barbara W. Keats. 1984. "Empirical Identification of the Criteria for Effective Affirmative Action Programs." *The Journal of Applied Behavioral Science* 20:203–22.

Hochschild, Jennifer. 1995. *Facing Up to the American Dream.* Princeton, NJ: Princeton University Press.

Holzer, Harry J. 1996. *What Employers Want.* New York: Russell Sage.

Holzer, Harry J. and David Neumark. Forthcoming 1998. "Are Affirmative Action Hires Less Qualified? Evidence from Employer-Employee Data on New Hires." *Journal of Labor Economics.*

Ibarra, Herminia. 1992. "Homophily and Differential Returns: Sex Differences in Network Structure and Access in an Advertising Firm." *Administrative Science Quarterly* 37:422–47.

———. 1993. "Personal Networks of Women and Minorities in Management: A Conceptual Framework." *Academy of Management Review* 18:46–87.

Jacobs, Jerry A. 1989. "Long-Term Trends in Occupational Segregation by Sex." *American Journal of Sociology* 95:160–73.

Jacobs, Jerry A. and Ronnie J. Steinberg. 1990. "Compensating Differentials and the Male-Female Wage Gap: Evidence from the New York State Comparable Worth Study." *Social Forces* 69:439–68.

Kalleberg, Arne L. and Barbara F. Reskin. 1995. "Gender Differences in Promotion in the United States and Norway." *Research in Social Stratification and Mobility* 14:237–64.

Kalleberg, Arne L., Edith Rasell, Naomi Cassirer, Barbara Reskin, Ken Hudson, David Webster, and Eileen Applebaum. 1997. *Nonstandard Work, Substandard Jobs.* Washington, DC: Economic Policy Institute.

Kanter, Rosabeth Moss. 1977. *Men and Women of the Corporation.* New York: Basic Books.

Kasinitz, Philip and Jay Rosenberg. 1996. "Missing the Connection: Social Isolation and Employment on the Brooklyn Waterfront." *Social Problems* 43:180–96.

Kelly, Erin and Frank Dobbin. 1998. "How Affirmative Action Became Diversity Management." *American Behavioral Scientist* 41:960–84.

Kennelly, Ivy. 1996. "'You've Got That Single-Mother Element': Employers' Images of African-American Women." Department of Sociology, University of Georgia, Athens, GA. Unpublished manuscript.

Kenney, Genevieve and Douglas Wissoker. 1994. "An Analysis of the Correlates of Discrimination Facing Young Hispanic Job-Seekers." *American Economic Review* 84:674–83.

Kern, Leesa. 1996. "Hiring and Seniority: Issues in Policing in the Post-Judicial Intervention Period." Department of Sociology, Ohio State University, Columbus, OH: Unpublished manuscript.

Kessler-Harris, Alice. 1982. *Out to Work.* New York: Oxford University Press.

Kirschenman, Joleen. 1996. "Skill Requirements and Employers' Gendered Perceptions of African-American Workers." Paper presented at a Conference on African-American and Latina Women in the Labor Market, Russell Sage Foundation, April 19–20, New York.

Kirschenman, Joleen and Kathryn M. Neckerman. 1991. "'We'd Love to Hire Them But ...' The Meaning of Race for Employers." Pp. 203–34 in *The Urban Underclass*, edited by C. Jencks and P. Peterson. Washington, DC: Brookings Institution.

Komaromy, Miriam; Kevin Grumbach, Michael Drake, Karen Vranizan, Nicole Lurie, Dennis Keane, and Andrew Bindman. 1996. "The Role of Black and Hispanic Physicians in Providing Health Care for Underserved Populations." *New England Journal of Medicine* 334:1305–10.

Konrad, Alison M. and Frank Linnehan. 1995a. "Formalized HRM Structures: Coordinating Equal Employment Opportunity or Concealing Organizational Practices?" *Academy of Management Journal* 38:787–820.

———. 1995b. "Race and Sex Differences in Line Managers' Reactions to Equal Employment Opportunity and Affirmative Action Interventions." *Group and Organization Management* 20:409–39.

Koski v. Gainer 1995. N.D. ILL., September 29, 1997.

Kraiger, Kurt and J. Kevin Ford. 1985. "A Meta-Analysis of Ratee Race Effects in Performance Ratings." *Journal of Applied Psychology* 70:56–65.

Kravitz, David A., David A. Harrison, Marlene E. Turner, Edward L. Levine, Wanda Chaves, Michael T. Brannick, Donna L. Denning, Craig J. Russell, and Maureen A. Conard. 1997. *Affirmative Action: A Review of Psychological and Behavioral Research.* Bowling Green, OH: Society for Industrial and Organizational Psychology.

Landau, Jacqueline. 1995. "The Relationship of Race and Gender to Managers' Ratings of Promotion Potential." *Journal of Organizational Behavior* 16:391–400.

LeBreton, Laurie W., Sara S. Loevy, and Lauren Sugerman. 1995. "Building Equal Opportunity. Six Affirmative Action Programs for Women Construction Workers." Chicago, IL: Chicago Women in the Trades.

Leonard, Jonathan S. 1984a. "The Impact of Affirmative Action on Employment." *Journal of Labor Economics* 2:439–63.

———. 1984b. "Employment and Occupational Advance under Affirmative Action." *The Review of Economics and Statistics* 66:377–85.

———. 1984c. "Anti-Discrimination or Reverse Discrimination: The Impact of Changing Demographics, Title VII, and Affirmative Action on Productivity." *Journal of Human Resources* 19:145–74.

———. 1985. "What Promises Are Worth? The Impact of Affirmative Action Goals." *Journal of Human Resources* 20:3–20.

———. 1987. "Affirmative Action." Working Paper, Spring, pp. 9–12, National Bureau of Economic Research, Chicago, IL.

———. 1990. "The Impact of Affirmative Action Regulation and Equal Employment Law on Black Employment." *Journal of Economic Perspectives* 4:47–63.

———. 1994. "Use of Enforcement Techniques in Eliminating Glass Ceiling Barriers." Report to the Glass Ceiling Commission, April, U.S. Department of Labor, Washington, DC.

Lichter, Daniel T. 1988. "Racial Differences in Underemployment in American Cities." *American Journal of Sociology* 93:771–92.

Lichter, Daniel T. and David J. Landry. 1991. "Labor Force Transitions and Underemployment: The Stratification of Male and Female Workers." *Research in Stratification and Social Mobility* 10:63–87.

Local 28 of the Sheet Metal Workers' International Association et al. v. Equal Employment Opportunity Commission et al., 478 U.S. 421 (1986).

Lovrich, Nicholas P., Brent S. Steel, and David Hood. 1986. "Equity versus Productivity: Affirmative Action and Municipal Police Services." *Public Productivity Review* 39:61–72.

Lynch, Frederick R. 1989. *Invisible Victims: White Males and the Crisis of Affirmative Action.* New York: Greenwood.

———. 1997. *The Diversity Machine: The Drive to Change the White Male Workplace.* New York: Free Press.

Major, Brenda, Jeffrey Feinstein, and Jennifer Crocker. 1994. "Attributional Ambiguity of Affirmative Action." *Basic and Applied Social Psychology* 15:113–41.

Markham, William T., Sharon L. Harlan, and Edward J. Hackett. 1987. "Promotion Opportunity in Organizations: Causes and Consequences." *Research in Personnel and Human Resources Management* 5:223–87

Marsden, Peter V. 1994. "The Hiring Process: Recruitment Methods." *American Behavioral Scientist* 7:979–91.

Martin, Susan E. 1991. "The Effectiveness of Affirmative Action: The Case of Women in Policing." *Justice Quarterly* 8:489–504.

Martocchio, Joseph J. and Ellen M. Whitener. 1992. "Fairness in Personnel Selection: A Meta-Analysis and Policy Implications." *Human Resources* 45:489–506.

Maryland Troopers Association Inc. v. Evans. 993 F.2d 1072 (1993).

Mayhew, Leon. 1968. *Law and Equal Opportunity: A Study of Massachusetts Commission against Discrimination.* Cambridge. MA: Harvard University Press.

McGinley, Ann C. 1997. "The Emerging Cronyism Defense and Affirmative Action: A Critical Perspective on the Distinction between Color Blind and Race-Conscious Decision Making Under Title VII." *Arizona Law Review* 39:1004–59.

McGuire, Gail M. 1998. "Do Race and Sex Affect Employees' Access to and Help from Mentors? Insights from the Study of a Large Corporation." Pp. 189–228 in *Mentoring Dilemmas: Developmental Relationships Within Multicultural Organizations*, edited by F. Crosby, R. Ely, and A. Murrell. Mahwah, NJ: Lawrence Erlbaum.

McGuire, Gail M. and Barbara F. Reskin. 1993. "Authority Hierarchies at Work: The Impacts of Race and Sex." *Gender & Society* 7:487–506.

McMillen, Liz. 1995. "[Affirmative Action] Policies Said to Help Companies Hire Qualified Workers at No Extra Cost." *Chronicle of Higher Education,* November 17, p. A7.

Messick, David M. and Dianne M. Mackie. 1989. "Intergroup Relations." *Annual Review of Psychology* 40:45–81.

Miller, Joanne. 1994. *Corporate Responses to Diversity: A Benchmark Study.* New York: Center for the New American Workforce, Queens College, City University of New York.

Miller, Shazia Rafiullah and James E. Rosenbaum. 1997. "Hiring in a Hobbesian World." *Work and Occupations* 24:498–523.

Moland, John, Jr. 1996. "Social Change, Social Inequality, and Intergroup Tensions." *Social Forces* 75:403–21.

Molyneux, Guy. 1996. "Recent Public Opinion Research on Race and Affirmative Action." Paper presented at GSS Conference on "Beyond Black and White: Multiculturalism and the General Social Survey," Washington, DC.

Moore, David W. 1995. "Americans Today Are Dubious about Affirmative Action." *The Gallup Poll Monthly*, March, pp. 36–8.

Moskos, Charles. 1996. "Affirmative Action in the Army: Why It Works." Pp. 227–38 in *The Affirmative Action Debate*, edited by G. E. Curry. Reading, MA: Addison-Wesley.

Moss, Philip and Chris Tilly. 1996. "'Soft' Skills and Race." *Work and Occupations* 23:252–76.

———. 1997. "Why Opportunity Isn't Knocking: Racial Inequality and the Demand for Labor." Department of Regional Economic and Social Development, University of Massachusetts, Lowell, MA. Unpublished manuscript.

Nacoste, Rupert Barnes. 1990. "Sources of Stigma: Analyzing the Psychology of Affirmative Action." *Law & Policy* 12:175–95.

Nay, Leslie A. and James E. Jones, Jr. 1989. "Equal Employment and Affirmative Action in Local Governments: A Profile." *Law and Inequality* 8:103–49.

Neckerman, Kathryn M. and Joleen Kirschenman. 1991. "Hiring Strategies, Racial Bias, and Inner-City Workers: An Investigation of Employers' Hiring Decisions." *Social Problems* 38:433–47.

Neumark, David. 1996. "Sex Discrimination in the Restaurant Industry: An Audit Study." *Quarterly Journal of Economics* 111:915–41.

Newman, Katherine S. 1996. "Job Availability." *National Forum* 76:20–23.

New York Times. 1995. "Reverse Discrimination Complaints Rare, Labor Study Reports." *New York Times,* March 31, p. A23.

Nieva, Veronica and Barbara A. Gutek. 1981. *Women and Work: A Psychological Perspective.* New York: Praeger.

Noble, Kenneth. 1986. "Employers Are Split on Affirmative Goals." *New York Times*, March 3, p. B4.

Norgren, Paul E. and Samuel E. Hill. 1964. *Toward Fair Employment*. New York: Columbia University Press.

Northrup, Herbert R. and John A. Larson. 1979. *The Impact of the AT&T-EEO Consent Decrees*. Labor Relations and Public Policy Series No. 20, University of Pennsylvania, Industrial Research Unit, Philadelphia, PA.

Norton, Eleanor Holmes. 1996. "Affirmative Action in the Workplace." Pp. 39–48 in *The Affirmative Action Debate*, edited by G. Curry. Reading, MA: Addison-Wesley.

OFFCP. See U.S. Department of Labor, Employment Standards Administration, Office of Federal Contract Compliance Programs.

O'Farrell, Brigid and Sharon Harlan. 1984. "Job Integration Strategies." Pp. 267–91 in *Sex Segregation in the Workplace: Trends, Explanations, and Remedies*, edited by B. Reskin. Washington, DC: National Academy Press.

Ohlott, Patricia J., Marian N. Ruderman, and Cynthia D. McCauley. 1994. "Gender Differences in Managers' Developmental Job Experiences." *Academy of Management Journal* 37:46–67.

O'Neill, Dave M. and June O'Neill. 1992. "Affirmative Action in the Labor Market." *Annals of the American Academy of Political and Social Science* 523:88–103.

Padavic, Irene A. 1991. "Attractions of Male Blue-Collar Jobs for Black and White Women: Economic Need, Exposure, and Attitudes." *Social Science Quarterly* 72:33–49.

Penn, Nolan E., Percy J. Russell, and Harold J. Simon. 1986. "Affirmative Action at Work: A Survey of Graduates of the University of California at San Diego Medical School." *American Journal of Public Health* 76:1144–46.

Petersen, Trond and Laurie A. Morgan. 1995. "Separate and Unequal: Occupation-Establishment Sex Segregation and the Gender Wage Gap." *American Journal of Sociology* 101:329–65.

Pettigrew, Thomas and Joanne Martin. 1987. "Shaping the Organizational Context for Black American Inclusion." *Journal of Social Issues* 43:41–78.

Pulakos, Elaine D., Leonard A. White, Scott L. Oppler, and Walter C. Borman. 1989. "Examination of Race and Sex Effects on Performance Ratings." *Journal of Applied Psychology* 74:770–80.

Quillian, Lincoln. 1995. "Prejudice as a Response to Perceived Group Threat: Population Composition and Anti-immigrant and Racial Prejudice in Europe." *American Sociological Review* 58:586–612.

Quirin v. City of Pittsburgh 1992, 801 F. Supp. 1486 (1992).

Ramirez, Albert. 1988. "Racism toward Hispanics: The Culturally Monolithic Society." Pp. 137–57 in *Eliminating Racism*, edited by P. A. Katz and D. A. Taylor. New York: Plenum.

Rand, A. Barry. 1996. "Diversity in Corporate America." Pp. 65–76 in *The Affirmative Action Debate*, edited by G. Curry. Reading, MA: Addison-Wesley.

Reskin, Barbara F. 1993. "Sex Segregation in the Workplace." *Annual Review of Sociology* 19:241–70.

Reskin, Barbara F. and Heidi Hartmann. 1986. *Women's Work, Men's Work: Sex Segregation on the Job*. Washington, DC: National Academy Press.

Reskin, Barbara F., Maureen Hickey, and Alusheyi Wheeler. 1998. "Trends in the Effects of Sex and Race on Intergroup Occupational Contact." Department of Sociology, Harvard University, Cambridge, MA. Unpublished manuscript.

Reskin, Barbara F. and Debra B. McBrier. 1998. "Why Not Ascription? Organizations' Employment of Male and Female Managers." Department of Sociology, Harvard University, Cambridge, MA. Unpublished manuscript.

Reskin, Barbara F. and Irene A. Padavic. 1988. "Supervisors as Gatekeepers: Male Supervisors' Response to Women's Integration in Plant Jobs." *Social Problems* 35:401–15.

————. 1994. *Women and Men at Work*. Thousand Oaks, CA: Pine Forge Press.

Reskin, Barbara F. and Patricia Roos. 1990. *Job Queues, Gender Queues*. Philadelphia, PA: Temple University Press.

Rhode, Deborah L. 1989. *Justice and Gender*. Cambridge, MA: Harvard University Press.

Rodgers, William and William E. Spriggs. 1996. "The Effect of Federal Contractor Status on Racial Differences in Establishment-Level Employment Shares: 1979–1992." *American Economic Association Papers and Proceedings* 86:290–3.

Roper Center for Public Opinion. 1995. *Poll Database:* Question ID USGALLUP.95MRW1.R32 [MRDF]. Storrs, CT: Roper Center for Public Opinion [producer, distributor].

Rosenbloom, David H. 1977. *Federal Equal Employment Opportunity*. New York: Praeger.

Sackett, Paul R., Cathy L. Z. DuBois, and Ann Wiggins Noe. 1991. "Tokenism in Performance Evaluation: The Effects of Work Groups' Representation on Male-Female and White-Black Differences in Performance Ratings." *Journal of Applied Psychology* 76:263–67.

Salancik, Gerald R. and Jeffrey Pfeffer. 1978. "Uncertainty, Secrecy, and the Choice of Similar Others." *Social Psychology* 41:246–55.

San Diego Union-Tribune. 1995. "Groups at Odds over Affirmative Action Revisions." *San Diego Union-Tribune,* September 13, p. AA-2.

Santoro, Wayne A. 1995. "Black Politics and Employment Policies: The Determinants of Local Government Affirmative Action." *Social Science Quarterly* 76:794–806.

Shaeffer, Ruth G. and Edith F. Lynton. 1979. "Corporate Experience in Improving Women's Job Opportunities." Report No. 755. The Conference Board, New York.

Schuman, Howard, Charlotte Steeh, Larry Bobo, and Maria Krysan. 1997. *Racial Attitudes in America: Trends and Interpretations.* Rev. ed. Cambridge, MA: Harvard University Press.

Shaw, Lois B., Dell P. Champlin, Heidi I. Hartmann, and Roberta M. Spalter-Roth. 1993. "The Impact of Restructuring and the Glass Ceiling on Minorities and Women." Report to the Glass Ceiling Commission, U.S. Department of Labor, Washington, DC.

Sigelman, Lee and Steven Tuch. 1997. "Metastereotypes: Blacks' Perceptions of Whites' Stereotypes of Blacks." *Public Opinion Quarterly 61*:87–101.

Skrentny, John David. 1996. *The Ironies of Affirmative Action: Politics, Culture, and Justice in America.* Chicago, IL: University of Chicago Press.

Smith, James P. and Finis Welch. 1984. "Affirmative Action and Labor Markets." *Journal of Labor Economics* 2:269–301.

Smith, Tom W. 1990. "Ethnic Images." General Social Survey Technical Report #19, National Opinion Research Center, Chicago, IL.

Sniderman, Paul M. and Thomas Piazza. 1993. *The Scar of Race.* Cambridge. MA: Harvard University Press.

Spalter-Roth, Roberta M., Arne L. Kalleberg, Edith Rasell, Naomi Cassirer, Barbara Reskin, Ken Hudson, David Webster, Eileen Applebaum, and Betty L. Dooley. 1997. *Managing Work and Family: Nonstandard Work Arrangements among Managers and Professionals.* Washington, DC: Economic Policy Institute.

Steeh, Charlotte and Maria Krysan. 1996. "The Polls—Trends: Affirmative Action and the Public, 1970–1995." *Public Opinion Quarterly* 60:128–58.

Steel, Brent S. and Nicholas P. Lovrich. 1987. "Equality and Efficiency Tradeoffs in Affirmative Action—Real or Imagined? The Case of Women in Policing." *Social Science Journal* 24:53–70.

Steinberg, Steven. 1995. *Turning Back: Retreat from Racial Justice in American Thought.* Boston, MA: Beacon.

Steele, Shelby. 1990. *The Content of Our Character*. New York: Basic Books.

Stephanopoulos, George and Christopher Edley, Jr. 1995. "Affirmative Action Review." Report to the President, Washington, DC.

Sutton, John R., Frank R. Dobbin, John W. Meyer and W. Richard Scott. 1994. "Legalization of the Workplace." *American Journal of Sociology* 99:944.

Taylor, Marylee C. 1994a. "Beliefs about the Preferential Hiring of Black Applicants: Sure It Happens, But I've Never Seen It." Pennsylvania State University, University Park, PA. Unpublished manuscript.

————. 1994b. "Impact of Affirmative Action on Beneficiary Groups: Evidence from the 1990 General Social Survey." *Basic and Applied Social Psychology* 15:143–78.

————. 1995. "White Backlash to Workplace Affirmative Action: Peril or Myth?" *Social Forces* 73:1385–1414.

Tetlock, Philip E. 1985. "Accountability: The Neglected Social Context of Judgment and Choice." Pp. 297–332 in *Research in Organizational Behavior*, vol. 7, edited by L. L. Cummings and B. M. Staw. Greenwich, CT: JAI Press.

————. 1992. "The Impact of Accountability on Judgment and Choice: Toward a Social Contingency Model." *Advances in Experimental Social Psychology* 25:331–76.

Tetlock, Philip and Jae I. Kim. 1987. "Accountability and Judgment Processes in a Personality Prediction Task." *Journal of Personality and Social Psychology* 52:700–709.

Thomas, Barbara. 1990. "Women's Gains in Insurance Sales." Pp. 183–204 in *Job Queues, Gender Queues*, by B. Reskin and P. A. Roos. Philadelphia, PA: Temple University Press.

Tomaskovic-Devey, Donald. 1993. *Gender and Racial Inequality at Work*. Cornell, NY: ILR Press.

Treiman, Donald J. and Kermit Terrell. 1975. "Women, Work, and Wage-Trends in the Female Occupational Structure." Pp. 157–200 in *Social Indicator Models*, edited by K. C. Land and S. Spilerman. New York: Russell Sage.

Turner, Margery A., Michael Fix, and Raymond J. Struyk. 1991. "Opportunities Denied, Opportunities Diminished." Report 91–9, The Urban Institute, Washington, DC.

Turner, Marlene E. and Anthony R. Pratkanis. 1994. "Affirmative Action as Help: A Review of Recipient Reactions to Preferential Selection and Affirmative Action." *Basic and Applied Social Psychology* 15:43–69.

Turner, Susan. 1996. "Barriers to a Better Break: Wages, Race, and Space in Metropolitan Detroit." Department of Sociology, Wayne State University, Detroit, MI. Unpublished manuscript.

U.S. Bureau of the Census. 1963. *Census of the Population and Housing, 1960*: Subject Report, Occupational Characteristics. PC(2)-7A. Washington, DC: U.S. Government Printing Office.

———. 1972. *Census of the Population and Housing, 1970*: Public Use Microsamples [MRDF]. Washington, DC: U.S. Bureau of the Census [producer].

———. 1973. *1970 Census of Population: Subject Reports, Occupational Characteristics.* Final Report PC(2)-7A. Washington, DC: U.S. Government Printing Office.

———. 1983. *Census of Population and Housing, 1980.* Public Use Microsamples [MRDF]. Washington, DC: U.S. Bureau of the Census [producer].

———. 1992. *Census of Population and Housing, 1990.* Public Use Microsamples [MRDF]. Washington, DC: U.S. Bureau of the Census [producer].

———. 1995. *Statistical Abstract of the United States: 1995.* 115th ed. Washington, DC: U.S. Government Printing Office.

———. 1998. *Statistical Abstracts of the United States, 1997.* Washington, DC: U.S. Department of Commerce. (CD-ROM, CD-COMP-ABSTR97)

U.S. Bureau of Labor Statistics. 1971. *Employment and Earnings* 18 (January). Washington, DC: U.S. Government Printing Office.

———. 1991. *Employment and Earnings* 38 (January). Washington, DC: U.S. Government Printing Office.

———. 1995a. "Contingent and Alternative Employment Arrangements." Report No. 900. Washington, DC: U.S. Government Printing Office.

———. 1995b. *Current Population Survey, Special Supplement on Contingent Work,* (February). Washington, DC: U.S. Government Printing Office.

———. 1996. *Employment and Earnings,* 42 (January). Washington, DC: U.S. Government Printing Office.

———. 1997. *Employment and Earnings* 43 (January). Washington, DC: U.S. Government Printing Office.

U.S. Commission on Civil Rights. 1981. *Affirmative Action in the 1980s: Dismantling the Process of Discrimination.* Clearinghouse Publication no. 70. Washington, DC: U.S. Government Printing Office.

U.S. Department of Labor. 1996. "The Facts on Executive Order 11246: Affirmative Action." Washington, DC: Office of Federal Contract Compliance Programs.

U.S. Department of Labor, Employment Standards Administration. 1996. "ESA Press Release: Gallatin, Tennessee, Manufacturer Order to Pay Nearly $250,000 in EEO Agreement with U.S. Labor Department." Washington, DC: U.S. Department of Labor.

U.S. Department of Labor, Employment Standards Administration, Office of Federal Contract Compliance Programs [cited as OFCCP]. n.d.(a) "Office of Federal Contract Compliance Programs Fact Sheet." Washington, DC: U. S. Department of Labor.

———. n.d.(b). "The Rhetoric and the Reality about Federal Affirmative Action at the OFCCP." Washington, DC: U. S. Department of Labor.

———. 1995. "Smith and Wesson, Inc. to Pay $450,00 in Back Wages in Gender Discrimination Case." Washington, DC: U. S. Department of Labor. Retrieved June 5, 1998 (http://www.dol.gov/dol/ofccp/esa/press/esa/esa95199.htm).

———. 1996. "OFCCP Egregious Discrimination Cases." November. Washington, DC: U. S. Department of Labor.

———. 1998a. "Affirmative Action at OFCCP: A Sound Policy and A Good Investment." Employment Standards Administration, Office of Federal Contract Compliance Programs, Washington, DC: U. S. Department of Labor. Retrieved April 16, 1998 (www.dol.gov/dol/esa/public/regs/compliance).

———. 1998b. "U.S. Department of Labor, Office of Federal Contract Compliance Programs, Quick Facts." Employment Standards Administration, Office of Federal Contract Compliance Programs, Washington, DC: U. S. Department of Labor. Retrieved June 9, 1998 (www.dol.gov/dol/esa/public/media/reports/ofccp/ofqfacts.htm).

U.S. Department of Labor, Office of Federal Contract Compliance Programs, Glass Ceiling Commission. 1995. *Good for Business: Making Full Use of the Nation's Human Capital/The Environmental Scar*. Washington, DC: U.S. Government Printing Office.

U.S. Department of Labor, Office of Federal Contract Compliance Programs. 1996. "The Facts on Executive Order 11246 Affirmative Action." Washington, DC: U.S. Department of Labor.

Van Velsor, Ellen and Martha W. Hughes-James. 1990. *Gender Differences in the Development of Managers: How Women Managers Learn from Experience*. Greensboro, NC: Center for Creative Leadership.

Verhovek, Sam Howe. 1997. "In Poll, Americans Reject Means but Not Ends of Racial Diversity." *New York Times*, December 14, pp.1,32.

117

Vernon-Gerstenfeld, Susan and Edmund Burke. 1985. "Affirmative Action in Nine Large Companies: A Field Study." *Personnel* 62:54–60.

Waldinger, Roger and Thomas Bailey. 1991. "The Continuing Significance of Race: Racial Conflict and Racial Discrimination in Construction." *Politics and Society* 19:291–323.

Wall Street Journal. 1979. "Labor Letter: A Special News Report on People and Their Jobs in Offices, Fields and Factories: Affirmative Action Is Accepted by Most Corporate Chiefs." *Wall Street Journal,* April 3, p. 1.

Wall Street Journal/NBC News Poll. 1996. Retrieved June 28 (http://interactive5.wsj.com/edition/resources/documents/ junepoll.htm).

Watson, Warren E., Kamalesh Kumar, and Larry K. Michaelsen. 1993. "Cultural Diversity's Impact on Interaction Process and Performance: Comparing Homogeneous and Diverse Task Groups." *Academy of Management Journal* 36:590–602.

White, Jack E. 1996. "Texaco's White-Collar Bigots." *Time,* November 18, p. 104.

Williams, John E. and Deborah L. Best. 1986. "Sex Stereotypes and Intergroup Relations." Pp. 244–59 in *Psychology of Intergroup Relations*, edited by S. Worchel and W. G. Austin. Chicago, IL: Nelson-Hall.

Wilson, William Julius. 1996. *When Work Disappears: The World of the New Urban Poor.* New York: Knopf.

Wright, Peter, Stephen P. Ferris, Janine S. Hiller, and Mark Kroll. 1995. "Competitiveness through Management of Diversity: Effects on Stock Price Valuation." *Academy of Management Journal* 38:272–87.

Zemsky, Robert and Maria Iannozzi. 1995. "A Reality Check: First Findings from the EQW National Employer Survey." *Issues* (10). National Center on the Educational Quality of the Workforce, University of Pennsylvania, Philadelphia, PA.

ABOUT THE AUTHOR

BARBARA F. RESKIN

Barbara F. Reskin completed her Ph.D. at the University of Washington in 1973. She is Professor of Sociology at Harvard University. Most of Reskin's research and teaching focus on sex, race, and ethnic inequality in employment. She has published several dozen articles and chapters on these topics along with five books, including *Women and Men at Work* (with Irene Padavic, 1994); *Job Queues, Gender Queues: Explaining Women's Inroads into Male Occupations* (with Patricia Roos, 1990), *Women's Work, Men's Work: Sex Segregation on the Job* (with Heidi Hartmann, 1986); *Sex Segregation in the Workplace: Trends, Explanations, Remedies* (1984), and *Sex Differences in the Professional Life Chances of Chemists* (1980). Reskin has served as Vice President of the American Sociological Association, chaired Committee W of the American Association of University Professors, was study director for the National Research Council's committee on Women's Employment, chaired the Organizations, Occupations, and Work Section of the American Sociological Association, and served as an expert witness in discrimination suits. She has been a Fellow at the Center for Advanced Study in the Behavioral Sciences, received the Distinguished Scholar Award from the American Sociological Association Section on Sex and Gender, and was a Lecturer in the Sociologists for Women in Society's series on Women and Social Change.

SOCIAL SCIENCE PERSPECTIVES ON AFFIRMATIVE ACTION

WORKSHOP PARTICIPANTS

American Sociological Association
June 27-29, 1996

Barbara Reskin (Convenor), Department of Sociology, Harvard University

William Bielby, Department of Sociology, University of California-Santa Barbara

Paul Burstein, Department of Sociology, University of Washington

Sharon Collins, Department of Sociology, University of Illinois-Chicago

Frank Dobbin, Department of Sociology, Princeton University

Lauren Edelman, Center for the Study of Law & Society, University of California- Berkeley

Edgar Epps, Professor of Urban Education, University of Chicago

Maureen Hallinan, Department of Sociology, University of Notre Dame

Jennifer Hochschild, Woodrow Wilson School, Princeton University

Carla B. Howery, Deputy Executive Officer, American Sociological Association

Allison Konrad, School of Business Management, Temple University

Jonathan Leonard, Haas School of Business, University of California-Berkeley

Felice J. Levine, Executive Officer, American Sociological Association

Thomas Pettigrew, Professor of Social Psychology, University of California-Santa Cruz

John Skrentny (Post-workshop Participant), Department of Sociology, University of Pennsylvania

Stephen Steinberg, Department of Urban Studies, Queens College-CUNY

Marylee Taylor, Department of Sociology, Pennsylvania State University